Beyond Wifi

Find your Deeper Connection

8 Ways to Be Refreshed Now

TIM MALONE, M.Div.

ISBN-13: 978-0-692-06805-2 (paperback)

ISBN-10 0-692-06805-8

Sources can be found at end of the book. All photos public domain except author page; property of himself.

Published through www.timmalone.org and Find your Deep Connection Retreat Center.
Note: The information in this book is intended as a sharing of experience and best practices that assisted the author in practical living choices. In no way is this book intended to replace, countermand or conflict with the advice given to you by your physician or mental health practitioner.

The ultimate decision concerning care should be made between you and your doctor. The information in this book is general and is offered with no guarantees on the part of the author or resources therein. The author and publisher disclaim all liability in connection with the use of this book.

DEDICATION

This book is dedicated to my family, parents and ancestors who carefully prepared a platform for me to stand on and then spread my wings to fly and go beyond what they could have imagined...

It is also dedicated to those in the service industries of all kinds - who commit day after day to giving and helping - yet are rarely uplifted to the same level as those in the burgeoning technology field; In gratitude, may these resources offer some balm, consolation and empowering support.

"Let us be refreshed now, in our daily life, and so become more capable of being the presence of loving care our struggling communities need."

CONTENTS

1: Self-Care Strategies Toward Balanced Living

PART 1 - ORIGINS & INSPIRATIONS:

This is a Toolbox to Refreshment and well-being. At least it has been for one person who found ways to avoid burnout and find what is life-giving for half a century. Here I humbly offer my experience, strength and hope. Who this tool box for? This is a book for all of us who don the (bittersweet) human experience. Yet it may be especially valuable to those in the helping field - where "burn out" is common - and taking breaks is less supported. For example, it may assist those of you in emotionally demanding roles and professions, including stay-at-home moms (and dads!), caregivers of an ill loved one - or passionate teachers and activists whose care goes outward (amidst ever changing, often flawed systems-institutions). In practicing tools in any arenas where self-care and inner connection can get lost in the pouring out of ourselves we are often loving of our neighbor more than ourselves. In modern times with a population burgeoning at the seams and sense of a disconnection from nurturing community many of us feel overwhelmed with the need around us. In companioning helpers one on one, in groups and on retreats I witness a rainbow after the storm of stress pulling us in so many directions; people are looking for ways to recycle and refresh our energies so we can sustainably tend to the ills of the world in a long term way. However, I have come to discover that we need an antidote for stress beyond what the allure of what wifi and screens seem to offer us. Yet for many of us these tools often become our "go to" relaxation tool. What to do? New studies and books are emerging to describe this malaise of living on overwhelm and what happens when untended. Recent terms abound such as "compassion fatigue," second hand trauma, empathy fatigue and even a new way to name the side effect of most of our time spent in the concrete jungle as "nature deficit disorder."

Whether we resonate with one of these descriptions or find them curious, most of us can say we experience "stress" in our daily life and that we might even see it has negative effects on our body, mind and spirit. Stress has been defined as that which pulls us in two directions, (or more than two!); a tension our bodies take in resulting in tightness or anxiety — and often at times causing illness or physical strain. The opposite of stress in the body is stillness and relaxation. And in my experience of over thirty years in the helping field one antidote to stress-filled tension is refreshment. What does it mean to be refreshed? We can press a button to "refresh" our computer browser or website yet how do we refresh ourselves - in our daily lives - as if we just had a good night sleep? If this was a TV commercial it may go something like this: "In just minutes, you can be refreshed, now! What if you are minutes away from refreshment,,, that lasts you until the next break and no matter where you are in the world. No cash or ATM needed (You don't have to buy it, because it doesn't cost money!) Sounds too good to be true?

The key to this book is an Affirmation and a real possibility: IN JUST MINUTES YOU COULD BE REFRESHED! Often I hear people saying, "if only i was ____, (home, done with this task, or in Hawaii) then I could be____. (happy, free, refreshed) What if we don't need to wait till we get OUT of this place or space (or get home or out of whatever situation you're in which is stress-filled or fin which w feel trapped) . We just need to KNOW we can be refreshed. And have a handy toolbox to draw from.

What I have noticed with clients and within my own life: Patterns develop for us until we are working for the weekend, or next vacation. We can't wait to break out, say to hell with it all for a while - go on that dream place or to the next big concert — and tell ourselves once we arrive there: "That will refresh me nicely!" While that may be true on some level, our minds expecting ONLY that can refresh us creates its own trap. What if you have the tools to get refreshed, in your belt, right now. What if with some reflection on your previous experience and a few tools in this book you can find a deeper connection - that de-stresses body, mind and spirit. Discovering this has been consoling and empowering for me. One truth I have had to wake up to over the years: The fantasy that we THINK we need to get somewhere else for long periods of downtime (often plugged in to some machine) can actually keep us even more in the grip of stress.

Its true we need to plan for nourishing time in our off days and moments when away from work, yet in my experience with clients and groups time and time again it's in this present moment when we become aware we NEED something different. That's when it's wise to listen, and act positively, if even for one minute. That's when these tools come in handy, immediately, when we are ready to be refreshed and re-centered, an oasis in our busy life available to us NOW.

SELF-CARE STRATEGIES FOR THRIVING:

WHAT IS SELF-CARE ? This is a new word in our dictionary as of last year. Caring for the self involves paying attention to the body, mind and emotions as if we were tending a small child or elderly relative — with love, compassion and full presence. Are self-care and distraction the same thing — or mutually exclusive? Or is it a matter of quality of fulfillment versus just getting by? Hmmm. Ah, that is a mystery of human nature as to why we would distract ourselves, or choose something else "easier" though it never really satisfies for long. (Another "Snickers," anyone?!) To give ourselves a break on this and offer some compassion, suffice to say we were all set up!

What I mean by that is that we came with certain "programs" through our conditioning. Each of us was born into a certain culture, lifestyle & family with habits we learned, many helpful to survive through the tumultuous journey of childhood. This happened by words, yet research is showing that more happened by witnessing caretakers / teachers behavior. This is often termed "imprinting" — ways of reacting and responding were mirrored to us, and these, whether helpful or unhelpful now, are always the built in default setting for when we are under stress, tension, or struggling with turmoil. In my experience, we will notice ourselves reaching for this, or doing that, almost unconsciously as the brain has been patterned this way. This comes out of development psychology and brain research in the late 20th century - which became the major I studied and the context of the practices that upheld my life in equilibrium after a major life-changing illness stopped me in my tracks..

The Dream for many of us is to step forward from the strong foundations our families lovingly prepared for us into a life of solidity and success: For most of my peers in college the attitude worked well enough; why slow down - or pause - when you can fly through life, without reflection, apparently without a care? Such is the way of youth, right?! Well for me, I had to have a veritable physical breakdown, while studying premedicine at a prestigious midwest college, to get me to pause. When a computer crashes, we fix it or go buy a new one. When I crashed, developing a rare pneumonia at age 19, and a colon one doctor said was like that of a 40 year old man, I had to change. Change what? I had to try on new behaviors and get help to choose sustainable actions based on acceptance of my limitations. In essence, I had to find a tool box of support, including practitioners both conventional and non-conventional. Even with this beginning disciplines my dream of serving overseas had to wait. After graduation I marvel that I found the widest possible array of support by following an inner voice to do an internship in the great Pacific Northwest. Sometimes it has to be that dramatic, for it to "take," to set us on a path that involves regular patches of "grounding" behavior — a cancer diagnosis, for example, or an accident can be a massive wake-up call. These dramatic experiences - or just plain burn out at work - mean facing the truth: the body has limitations as well as gifts and talents, and these experiences are a call to honoring how we are built. In a way its about respecting the way we have been created. An early version of this book was aptly named; The Manual that goes with this human! Many years of trying out new different self-care techniques can be exhausting in and of itself — until we find the ones that fit like a glove. For me, all of the tools in this book have literally saved my life, time and time again. I come to remember these — that is, I try them on in new circumstances of my life. For example, when a transition happened some time ago I had to try them again - as if for the first time. A new job, a new living situation and new routines may distract us to forget the original healthy habits we put into place. I had to re-affirm them in the different context with creative vision and vigor, support and a conscious effort.

My own story of a young life without these led to an initial crash. Regularly going into portals of refreshment meant I didn't have to have a second crash in life, just a wiser soul adapting to new conditions. In all honesty, the movement to focus on what I need & want, to live a life in harmony. I have learned this must involve regular periods of balancing work and play, service and nurturing rest. For me this is still a life-long quest. What I find day after day in my service work with individuals and retreats has become the theme of these writings: Many people who come to me are asking a subterranean question without words: Is there a "deeper connection" (beyond wifi) which will truly refresh and sustain the busy pace of life with its responsibilities, obligations, and surprise invitations to growth?

In the self-assessment below you are invited to explore this question from your own graced history. The chapters which follow are my best practices for FINDING A

DEEPER CONNECTION ... to

— your joy, and to what your body might be inviting you to pay attention to,

— that which matters most to you, people, spaces, the source of your life,

— "true" and real self, beyond expectations demands, roles, i.e. to nature & your place on the earth,

— your purpose, the why you are here, at this time in the cosmos,

— your heart, that is, to discover and know your core emotions,

— be present to your family in re-newed ways,

— your natural style of living, your authentic life-style & pace,

— your vibrant spirit underneath the responsible woman / man,
— the wild, beautiful you some people may not even know (yet!),

— what gives you life, makes you feel alive,

— freedom and ease

— health & well-being

— to the ground of your being,

— that transcendent horizon we seek, the higher /bigger power and force many call by different names — Spirit or God - or Oneness of all Life.

A NOTE ABOUT THE FORM and FORMAT OF THIS MANUAL:

This book has been gestating and simmering in me for many years - in one form or another - as I stepped into various roles as a helping professional myself over the last 30 years and now it is time. The contents consist of the fruit of a lifetime of living, and thriving, because of finding and taking up these "tools" on a regular basis, especially when stressed or overwhelmed. I know they work to take me home to the deepest connection I know. Some will find the book form most helpful yet there will be the audio CD / for those who learn and try on by hearing a voice or seeing in action. Yet the benefit of the book is it fills out the why and therefore, the process and the links between each exercise. This is both a first volume of tried and true practices and as you will see, the first part of a compendium or process which has levels that I have personally moved through in refreshing my whole self to awaken. The hinge point is to present the exercises in language that is accessible and modern yet deeply applicable to any age. These tools are ready to pick up and start right away without need of a binding tradition or school or guru. (I'm certainly not interested in being any one's guru!) At the same time, some you may recognize their origin as ancient, powerful portals into refreshing and anchoring ourselves in the present moment and in our bodies as the only vehicle we really own for this whole life thus, the medium to truly, amazingly connect to the Source of our lives. If you practice within a tradition or community, these tools are inexhaustible connectors for you - like living streams of water, which refresh us utterly, almost unexpectedly. Within are the LEVEL 1 brief, daily exercises that you can pick up a few minutes a day. These are the building blocks which are enough to begin with, and yet, as most things which are profoundly worth it, can be deepened after laying the foundation. One image for trying these on is to plant them in your life and let them grow. The vision of a beginner's garden looking toward springtime, after being consistently cultivated and nurtured, becomes like wildflowers in bloom upon a mountainside or lush vegetables in a greenhouse in winter, yet this time, the garden is you.

PART 2 - EXERCISES & GUIDED MEDITATIONS

The Format of the *MODERN TOOL BOX OF HOPE* manual comprises two main parts within each chapter:

1. Origins and Inspirations which formed the author to put into action his values and best practices.

2. Exercises and uplifting Meditations to read or say out loud.

This second part introduces you to a 1-5 minute practice which is meant to be adapted in your daily life. Closing each chapter are reflection questions and a link to Song / meditations on the CD

A NOTE ON REFLECTION QUESTIONS:

One of the reasons I have included reflection questions is it that the process of stepping back and considering with some distance is itself an effective tool to discover more about ourselves. One key quality which distinguishes us from animals is our capacity to self-reflect and then consciously change our course of action or thought from this reference point. As was noted before, the imprinted patterns we carry, often not even chosen consciously, still operate. As adults we re-affirm these over and over again, often without any thought until we reflect. Then, with reflection we see — "Oh, my parent or guardian did that," and we can go back a generation to see, "Oh wow, so did grandma & grandpa" (their dad or mom), and so on. The point here is that now we get to pause, notice, and see we have choices — to continue this if it works for you - or to change, to shift whatever is no longer working for us - in every area of our life. This is our birthright. I can choose whether I really need Coke or Pepsi — or even more profoundly, how many minutes a day I might come back to my center, to get in touch with the real thing, full-being refreshment. In this book each practice carries with it a complementary song & poem, which may aid going into the heart of the intention and receive a surround sound type of refreshment you may be seeking. Playing your own favorite songs while trying on the exercise further enhances the 3-D experience, if that's how you want to roll with it.

So what what can really, truly refresh me now?

What has the capacity to refresh, restart my whole being into its original state of ease, (as if we could get our original owners manual on how to operate this thing called me!) This is actually the purpose of such exercises. By the end of this book and your trying on each one you get to confidently answer this question by naming the way that works best for you, AND claiming what style of applying these works best for you at this time (and others you've already discovered along the way). In this way you find your deeper connection, beyond wifi, for as many moments of your day or weekend, and as long as it fits you. This is ours to do. No one can do it for us. We get to refresh ... ourselves! Talk about habits as private victories and building self-esteem.

A NOTE ON HONORING OUR BODIES AND APPLICATION OF THE EXERCISES ANYWHERE WE FIND OURSELVES:. INVITE YOU TO CONSIDER

The 3 positions — Most likely to engage the practices:

1. SITTING:

~ An opportunity for just Be-ing.

~ As the old phrase goes in reverse; "don't just do something, sit, here, now."

2. STANDING:

~ tall as a tree

~ in your center of power

3. WALKING

~ Movement as meditation and exercise ` Shifts our

emotion states in positive direction

4. EXERCISE REGIMEN:
~ Some can be adapted for exercising, running or moments in between stretching, or even at the gym)

5. ERRANDS:

~ Almost all of these tools can be practiced sitting or standing, in line at a store or gas station, even at meetings for example, and most can be brought into your walking routine (some even as you walk your pet).

A SELF-ASSESSMENT ON REFRESHMENT IN OUR LIVES NOW

How do you get refreshed, now (beyond wifi ...) ??

At the heart of this book is a Quest:

To live mindfully, loving, sustainably in a way that brings refreshment to ourselves - and gets passed onto others (whom we encounter along the way). These are inextricably bound together, as the best of our ancient traditions illuminate. Yet practically speaking, our toolboxes are now in the form of machines - that is by this modern world of devices and distractions we can purchase. Most other voices or wisdom traditions are drowned out or relegated to one weekend hour of focus — or lost altogether. How might we "get refreshed" and renewed even in our busy times? To delve into the title of this chapter we first must ponder these questions:

• What *already* helps us to be mindful, and even loving, in our full schedules, with demands, (given opportunities are endlessly offered by our consumer culture and circle of friends, family, needs and hobbies?)

• What might refresh me now, at this stage in my life, with its unique set of roles, life style, and routines?

So let's do a little exercise together, shall we? Let's reflect on what this looks like, for me to be refreshed:

1. So what is *refreshment*?

> ~ What does this word mean to you ... feel like, look like?

~ When have you experienced this in the last month or season? (outside of a beverage or screen or shower or a good night's sleep). Scribble on this page, or write on a pad of paper or journal.

2. what does *"getting refreshed"* mean to you, in a word, or image ... a picture of yourself? (draw or make a face of helpful)

3. Synonyms: what are some other words for this or ways of usage in your language:

_____ RE- fresh refresh

browser fresh ness

suggestions: restore, reframe, release, re-lax, rest, restart, invigorate, energize.

4. What are common ways YOU refresh — at work, at home, in car, or on vacation?

Which ones cost $$? and which are freely accessible?

For example, most culturally sanctioned "refreshment" almost ALWAYS involves exchange of money $$. Advertisers and marketers use these words above to sell something manufactured, (usually with artificial ingredients or chemicals) such as a soft drink (sugar carbonated bubbles do the trick) calling it "the real thing" or "naturally refreshing." (Then why do we have to pay for it?!). Another example is scented products which refresh — even pine sol is pitched as a "refreshing scent" while you clean the floor or bathroom toilet!

5. What are one or two things you LOVE to do?

When is the last time you did that thing you love to do?

6. The NEXT STEP is speaking it out loud:

SHARE WITH A FRIEND OR LOVED ONE, WHAT YOU NAMED HERE, "WHAT REFRESHES YOU," AND CONSIDER TAKING A STEP FORWARD IN GIVING YOURSELF THIS GIFT SOON.

This following exercise is a prelude and introduction to the next chapter which focuses on the natural gift of breathing in refreshment.

ONE MINUTE TO REFRESHMENT

In any position and in any place you find yourself in - sitting, standing, walking, with others or alone -

we stop whatever we are doing with our minds and hands. To begin we take a deep breath, breathing nourishment in and breathing out what is no longer needed.

In the Next inhale, from your chest take in even more air than the previous time and then release out, letting it flow out like air out of a balloon.

Lastly, pause a moment or two, then from our bellies we draw a big breath in and pause a moment, before releasing it slowly

to the point we feel our shoulders relax and arms drop a little. Relax into ease and wellbeing.

Savor for a few moments.

That only took one minute, really!

APPLICATION INTO DAILY LIFE:

Now pick a tune which you know refreshes you in some way — it can be pop or classic, meditation, or inspirational song. Hum or sing it at the end of the breathing exercise or use it as background for the exercise and your transition to the next task of the day. If you're feeling particularly wound up or agitated, then repeat if helpful, preferably sitting down, eyes closed & well supported.

Remind yourself of the ways which you derive real refreshment, and consider making a habit out of one of these each time we transition seasons.

Breathe ... Find your Deep Connection ...

2: Three Breaths to Life

PART 1 - ORIGINS & INSPIRATIONS:

In this chapter we will explore the this first portal in depth and reflect on why such a simple thing as conscious breathing is important yet so challenging in this day and age. Simply Breathe, to Refresh. Naturally. Why this one, especially, first? Breathing seems so basic, so simple, as we All are breathing, all the time. Yet ironically while under duress this is the first to go...shallow. When in fight or flight mode, we actually stop breathing for a moment. We freeze.

Most of us in stressful jobs and family situations are really not getting the full oxygen our brains need to function in this challenging moment. That's why it's #1 on this list, actually, and for our bodies functioning, this is foundational. What if it takes only seconds, less than a minute, to return to a state where our shoulders relax a little, and sighs arise. With three deep breaths all of us settle into some more inner calm: blood pressure lowers and the mind always follows. In my experience even if we have racing thoughts, within 3-5 minutes of conscious breathing we can be refreshed, for the next hour of work or family engagement or sporting activity. So what if this breathing meditation / prayer must be named as a "skill," as are ABC's and arithmetic: we don't come with "habitual excellence" around this one, at least not in the West! Maybe that's why mindful meditation and stress reduction training is so popular- it has its own magazines and apps and YouTube videos now. The simple secret of all these techniques? It always involves breathing techniques at the front end. Anything after builds on first this step. In fact if you have even done Yoga or taken birth preparation classes, the same is true. It's about intentional awareness on breathing in and out, while focusing on a particular area of one's body. In fact, in the last few years it has become mandatory training for paramedics, fire and police officers, and even soldiers! They call it "tactical breathing!" So we are in good company with this modern realization that we are all walking around essentially as "shallow breathers," to use a phrase from MBSR (Mindfulness Based Stress Reduction) which I was trained in twenty years ago. I was a young mental health counselor in a community outpatient setting when this all come out in the 90's. And something inside me leapt at the chance to be one of the first in our center to apply them as part of our group therapy and treatment planning with persons suffering from chronic mental illnesses. Even then, before I had studied graduate theology and spirituality, I sensed this was something deeply missing and essential. In a sense it is a cross over from what ancient doctors and our chaplains have probably encouraged for many years: when under stress or anxious or in full of grief, first remember to breathe. Take a breath break.

The other reason we start with this one? Because Breathing is so basic we take it for granted, yet also because the pace of life is vastly different than even twenty years ago, before the age of internet and cell phones. In the agricultural societies of the West up until 150 years ago as well as other cultures in the east there was ample time for breathing. Often whole families spent hours resting on porches - or telling stories, before warming fires, especially after the harvest and when the land lay fallow. Research is revealing that the constant stimulation and potential for sixteen hours daily of intense electrical stimulation input into our nervous systems directly - through earbuds, portable screens, bluetooth - leave our bodies in a perpetual state of alertness. It is unparalleled in the history of human race. We are scarcely aware of it. We just keep plugging in. And wondering why our eyes are tired, sleep is disturbed and our brain seems always on overload. In 2018 we literally can dis-associate from our bodies to live in our rational intellects (a very small part of our brain), unplugging only to eat. Here is how it works physiologically: the demand for more oxygen means more inhaling is needed, yet mostly comes in gulps unless we are on a break and choosing to focus all of our attention on this activity of breathing. Secondly, if we are not breathing from our diaphragms where the majority of oxygen can be drawn up from then we are taking up limited nutrients. I used to teach clients in groups that only by breathing from down deep into our bellies we can we refresh our brains with a full intake of life-giving air. That is why we are essentially born into a culture of shallow breathers. This is why Yoga is so popular — it's all about the breath. Only then to attempt the stretch, right?! There are vast spiritual reasons for all this as well and it's deep in every major religious tradition. Yet we may notice today, in churches and temples, the Breath of Life origins were often forgotten nor passed on as a practical style of connection with a higher power. It's funny how our predominantly Christian culture could not see this in its own contemplative roots. Thus, so many millions of people have sought it in forms from the east such as Yoga (Hindu) and mindfulness (Buddhist roots). Practices from the the Christian contemplative tradition have this in common with the east: it almost always begins with the breath, and often silence for at least one minute. Now it's as if it's new - it's all the rage and people are branding their own style of it to make gobs of money, yet at it's core it's all the same, simple origins, and doesn't cost a thing. Breath is Life. In and out. Simply, profoundly refreshing. However, conscious breathing is not easy an easy habit to maintain yet in my experience it's so essential that I had to have a graduate school clinical professor remind me almost every class, "Tim, remember to breathe." How could she see that I was under so much stress I wasn't breathing all the air available to me? At age 26 this would be a major wake-up call to health and well being. Even before technological devices like cell phones I was running around out of breath. If it was tough to breathe deep in those times that what might it mean for us today, walking down the street, to our cars, (and everywhere else) with our eyes glued to our phone screens. What I realize this means, in practice, is that this needs to be named and claimed as the first real remedy to stress - and the fundamental portal to refresh. All the others in this book are build on this crucial life-giving foundation.

HANDY TOOLS — FINDING A SUSTAINABLE RELATIONSHIP WITH TECHNOLOGY

There were a number of 1970s English bands who wrote thoughtful and sometimes almost (accidentally?) meditational music. I grew up on artists like this and found refreshment in listening to radio or albums to the point that I became a DJ on college radio and an FM station before it became computerized. Thus, even though I have commented in this chapter on the shadow side of our beloved tools and machines of convenience I have a disclaimer and a note on technology: I love it and am intrigued by how it brings conveniences into my life. I seem to need it - and like many of us - music and images of beauty inspire and help us to cope with life's challenges. I grew up watching TV shows after school for as long as i can remember, and I have a great respect for science coming from the space program into our homes and vehicles, like being able to fly half way across the world in the same comfort as a commuter train. First of all, though chapter one strongly suggested an approach to unplug from devices I'm the first to admit how captivated I am with the next new phone with a great camera - or noise canceling- headphones for airports and cafes. Once I even spent nearly $1000 on a new car stereo back in the 1990's. I love movies on the big screen (with popcorn!) and am fascinated with amazing new safety features in rental cars like screens which show you such a clear back up radius. In fact, what I notice about myself is that every time I see a screen in a restaurant or a home my eyes go back to it again and again. Thus, I'm often distracted, yet I've been conditioned well; there is new information so readily available that I just get curious and wonder if I might miss out on something. Sigh. So, is there too much of a good thing?

At the same time i also notice its hold on me, and my need to step away regularly - or else it consumes all of my time and energy. Might this resonate with your experience at times? Your kids or grandkids, nieces and nephews, spouse? What I have come to realize it this: If I'm no longer choosing it — then it becomes the "default "- in the home, car and everywhere I go. Sometimes I wonder why I'm exhausted. Could it be from all the stimulation, all the time? Wondering why I am always so tired? When I ask one friend in my life about how he is feeling he always answers the same way: "I'm tired - since the day I was born." He has worked in the technology field his whole life and been constantly in front of a computer since junior high school - or a video game. Still is. I heave a great sigh when I'm back home with no TV, or other machines on, for my senses to absorb. It is literally a sigh of relief. I can take a breath. Whew - no new information is assaulting my senses. For this is the truth no company ever acknowledges: every input is in need of being processed by the brain (and every machine needs to be tended to - at least charged daily- like a little pet!). So much so I can't breathe. And sometimes I come home, just yawn and sit in the dark for ten minutes, finally stopping, getting a chance to breathe. Sometimes after a really challenging traffic commute I take a shower and go to bed.

One question which led to the genesis of this book: **Is there a connection for you between how much stimulation you take in and how tired you feel?** At what point are our eyes and brain crying out, "Enough!" It's time we took stock and considered that It is a new age. It's been less than seventy years with screens and instant input into our nervous systems. Yet the pace has redoubled every generation and even faster since the dawn of cell phones. So the question becomes both how to receive benefit from these as "tools" while striking a balance.. And what activity can fill its place — and really satisfy — our needs as a thriving human beings? If I'm just surviving - working in the coal mines - and living by the "another day, another dollar" adage — then video games, TV, beer, and other tools for mind-numbing may be just the ticket. Yet a fully lived life requires something more than eating, shopping, being plugged into these screens and phones - and church / synagogue on Sunday. It requires conscious habits which maybe only we can begin and only we ourselves can validate over time. Certainly if it can't be bought on Amazon it probably won't be encouraged — unless our spouse/ partner / community supports a counter-cultural approach with wisdom shared and ritualized and practiced. What we are talking about here is a sustainable lifestyle — based on reflection of what may nurture and nourish - through a connection beyond wifi, beyond the screens we are now so habitually reaching for. The tide is turning now that there is an official 12 step group many young people are attending to recover from this new attachment to screens called "Tech Addiction." There is hope that we are waking up to the benefits and pitfalls - of these devices and in that there is a new world of possibility.

As you read this what is your experience of these many tools of technology?

The sober truth: most of our available entertainment runs on intensity, adrenaline, excitement — and fear — manipulated, for our pleasure. This wasn't the case thirty years ago, certainly not before the age of the screen or boob tube, as it was called in the 1950's when it came out. Most of what we now call "getting connected," is only fifteen to twenty years old in the USA. Yet it's become the only way we know to turn off, check out, take a break, with a coke or coffee or beer (caffeine/sugar stimulant or alcoholic beverage depressant) to send us somewhere else — just not here. Anything to tune out after what I'm feeling after a long day at _____(work, kids, school, etc. you get to fill in the blank.) Mmmm finally refreshment. In my humble, susceptible experience guess what? They got us. It's all of us doing the same thing to try to "get refreshed -" yet is it working? Really? and how do we tell? With all due respect to the demands of our lives almost all of us like adrenaline, the intensity, the rush, the high it's like a flush of our system that puts us in touch with the moment, although it is enhanced - and comes at a cost to our body. Apparently we weren't made to be in hyper vigilant mode. What we used to call fight or flight, actually gets induced. What if it is really just fear and excitement pumped in - which cannot be sustained without body rest at some later time - nap or crashed out - or as we see in due seasons, we get sick. Sometimes it lasts three weeks. Our immune systems become compromised. Then the hit comes from a virus and we are forced into an uncomfortable position. Exercise is a good thing, and yet if its purpose is to get the high or boost the image (subconsciously) , we aren't really in the moment, but in the future. Our body is the tool - we use it to get something (or someone!) else. What happens to us when we are so stimulated, running on intensity and adrenaline pumping many hours a day? Fun. Happy. Intense. joy and play? The virtues of Joy and a truly refreshing play need to be distinguished from instant happiness and pleasure as the latter often involves excitement, stimulation, and intensity. There is a fine line between pleasure and high anxiety. Especially for our five senses - the real tool that these machines feed on. This brings us back to our topic of the breath. When we fire on all cylinders for much of day, we cannot but be shallow breathers. We rarely are getting the full oxygen we need. Over time our blood pressure may get so affected we may get woozy or dizzy. Yet the main invisible byproduct is we are unable to be fully present to what is in front of us, much less who. Then we treat each other as so many tasks, or as annoying interruptions to our imagined happy (and more and more mechanized day). We are creating a society of shallow breathers with new ones made every day by high pressured school and work environments in intensely crushed positions before a Holy temple of the Screen. With a prettier picture for the future, here I lay out the first portal which serves as foundation for all the others to come each chapter. What if we were made to just breathe, offer service and live? Breathe and Live. What if were were invited to be and live in relative peace — after our basic survival needs were met? As the first peoples of this land often name as a forward looking value: It is for the next generations, our children and the next seven generations that I write these words. My body gave out under tremendous pressure at age 19 before the dawn of screens at our fingertips. What will it be like for them?

PART 2: EXERCISES & GUIDED MEDITATIONS

A. The Three Breaths Portal to Refresh

So let us try these Exercises below. The first one is especially helpful when we only have 30 seconds to spare. "This will only take a minute," we can say to a co-worker (or friend or spouse), as we take a much-needed chance to locate ourselves.

In any position, in any place you find yourself in - sitting, standing, walking, working

we cease whatever we are doing with our minds and our hands.

Let us become aware of this precious moment, this opportunity to receive refreshment

and an inner connection.

To begin we take one deep breath:

Breathing in to refresh

and then breathing out what is no longer needed.

These phrases may assist you to focus the mind on the breath:

Breathe in Refreshment,

Breathe out, Worries.

Continuing with the above phrase (if helpful), we inhale again from our diaphragm and

then release out, being freed from burdens we may not even know we are carrying.

B. Find our deeper connection to Life

If you have a minute or two, then jump right in and add the next exercise in an undistracted place for you to take a break:

In sitting position, preferably in a straight-backed chair, enter a posture which allows you to be comfortable yet alert. It is best for the body to be held with the back well supported and hands in position of rest on the lap, or open to receiving. After entering the Three Breaths Portal (above #1), we allow ourselves to breathe normally, through our nose, without pushing or straining. This time, as we breathe in and breathe out, we imagine being filled up with the freshness of life, of what it has to offer.

Let us gently allow the in-breath to fill us up with this precious oxygen. and release the byproducts out of our system.

Next, we let the air out slowly, gently encouraging each exhale a little bit longer.

If helpful, we can count so that the "in breath" is 1, 2, 3
then the exhale is 4, 5, 6, and 7. Let your chests expand naturally with this nudge to greater numbers as suits our lungs capacity.

Continuing Breathing this way and if your mind wanders, try counting inward again or even out loud, or coming back to the image suggested of filling up with freshness.

C. Visualize, Harmonize & Release

Breathing in, I'm Being Filled
Breathing out, I'm Refreshed!

What follows is an opportunity for breathing with deeper consciousness of our interconnectedness to all that is around us. It's a way to receive and naturally give in return. We might visualize receiving precious nutrients from the rich abundance of our atmosphere. We connect to our habitat with its blooms and blue sky while releasing nourishing carbon dioxide back to the earth, especially the trees, plants, in a syncopation of harmony, into right relationship on the planet. This is one thing we can do to give back, however small it may seem. Continue conscious breathing and when we notice uncomfortable stuff coming up to be released then in the out breath let out a SIGH, even with a sound or a groan. Another way to release the pent up energy trapped in us is by taking what I call a BLUBBER BREATH. That is, letting the breath release from the lips in a sound that starts with a "B." It is reminiscent of a child blowing bubbles with her mouth or the steam escaping out of a pipe. In my experience this tool naturally frees us from built up tension, including frustration, disappointment and other strong emotions we often may carry through our long days. Try this with a playful attitude and see what happens. It may be you have already been doing it in stressful moments and not realized until now.

APPLICATION IN DAILY LIFE : The One Minute Morning Wake-up Breath:

This very simple exercise is actually quite ancient, if largely forgotten. It is said if we take three breaths in the morning we are guaranteed to be on the path to mindful practice the rest of the day. (This wisdom relayed to me on my one year solo Himalayan pilgrimage in the year 2000.) Since then I practice this each day when alarm sounds. At the moment we wake up immediately, lovingly take three deep breaths as the first thing we do before getting out of bed. Before grabbing the phone or turning off the clock radio. This has been encouraged by Ayurvedic health doctors for more than three millennia. Lastly, most cell phones now have multiple alarm settings. Allow this modern tool to help us remember to take three refreshing breaths arranged throughout the day. Much of this chapter is inspired from the traditions of mindfulness over hundreds of centuries along with Mindful Based Stress Reduction (MBSR). The exercises above have been informed by many years at practice centers around the world yet invite you to begin with www.plumvillage.org as this has been a major factor in my learning and great next step to consider.

A SONG from the Tim Malone & SOUL FAM CD …A most excellent help to our centering ourselves and as a bonus soundtrack for your breathing consider listening to track 10 of the Tim Malone & Soul Fam CD - or on find on Youtube titled, "Total Harmonic Convergence." The relaxing sound of the harmonics on the guitar are not unlike bells, which take us deeper in our connection to ourselves and to the present moment. Or what other another musical accompaniment might you enjoy. For example, put on a favorite instrumental track on earbud, or home / car stereo and let this accompany you into opening up to spaciousness ... in your life. Hmm, so good.

Questions For Reflection:

Q. 1 Why might this be helpful, to start out my day? (even before we put the coffee machine on). Alternatively, what happens when you literally jump out of bed into your day - in a bit of a rush — and don't first take a moment?

Q. 2 What would happen if you practiced three breaths regularly such as on a break time or scheduled it before of after work /errands. What difference might this make for you?

Q. 3 What difference might this make for those around you; your family, co-workers, neighbors, in the car beside you in traffic, and even your pets? ;)

Consider writing in a stream of conscious your answers to the above. Ponder what you discover.

3: Press Pause and Notice

A Poem, a morning routine,
Portals to Refreshment any time of day:

Breathe....

(Press) Pause. What do you Notice?

Be Still, and Know:

Listen, Now, Your Heart opens,

When
Connecting

To Gratitude
in your Deep Being;

To Nature, to Ancestors

And to the Source of Love.

Where we Find Creative Energy,

We Come Home to Ourselves

And Become a Loving presence in the World.

PART 1 - ORIGINS & INSPIRATIONS:

This whole manual book is an unpacking of the prayer-poem above — all the exercises - or portals as I am naming them. Continuing to build the foundation in simple ways: This chapter has a number of pivot points, for reflection, and invites us to continue making simple habits of finding deeper connection beyond wifi. One portal to Refreshment is certainly the act of "Pressing Pause" during our busy days. The first two Chapter's exercises can be combined with this new one seamlessly. The second half of the avenue to Press Pause is the question, "What do you Notice?" Here I introduce a tool for individuals and groups that I have utilized for over twenty years called, "The Weather Report." The great value of pausing and having a "look-see" at what we notice within and around us is not just for ourselves - it has positive repercussions for all those we encounter that day.

Pause for a moment.

I use the phrase "Press Pause" as it has a meaning in today's culture which is almost universal. Almost any electronic device, even our car's stereo, comes with this feature. For example, when I listen to music or watch a movie on a device I often fall into the stream of its hypnotic unfolding. This reverie continues until something comes up to pull me out — a phone call or another's voice or ring at the door. Or I wake up to a want or need from inside me. I may want to grab a beverage or food, for example, or need to go to the bathroom. Then I press the pause button. So often it's a rush to go do that task so I can get back to the media I'm engrossed in. The kind of "Pressing Pause" that I have learned I need is something a little broader yet the catch phrase applies. This pausing isn't just to go get something or complete a task so I can resume the entertainment. This chapter's exercises and suggestions open up an invitation. Invitation to what? To wake up to the moment and see what it holds. Essentially, I take a "connect break." The double meaning inherent is that I'm freeing myself from one kind of connection to open up to another. I wake up to having a choice among infinite options in my life as to what will serve and refresh me. I have come back to being a human rather than a human doing. Thus, it is less about "doing" something when I press pause and more about "being." Just being. (Here, now.)

Human Anthropology 501: The origins of pausing, and noticing lie in the nature of being a human. What distinguishes us from animals is precisely that we can rely on instinct when necessary yet be self-aware enough to pause and consider other options. If I am self-aware then I can pause and reflect. A rich world of choices opens up to me. The capacity for human self-understanding and living beyond the fight or flight or freeze reaction is a tremendous gift — and often taken for granted.

The fact that I can respond as an actor in my life rather than a reactor needs remembering, and is often lost on us, especially if we live at a fast pace. It is humbling to acknowledge that most of our species is still in a process somewhere between our animal nature and this human potential. It is good medicine to come back to the here and the now. Yet like like any healthy habit, it requires some intention and practice. And patience. And compassion for myself. Why? It's going against the inertia and there will resistance, inner and outer. In this day and age, Pressing pause is a radical act of waking and of snapping out of the spell our world weaves daily. I liken it a kind of mass agreement to keep moving onto the next sound bite, what I call "entertainment hypnosis." Pause-ing means opening our eyes to what is. The ancient traditions remind us that by beginning again with the Breath we regain access to a moment of presence. We return to be true-ly present to the moment we are in. This is the genius of the mindfulness movement, of Yoga, of Christian Contemplative Prayer styles and The Spiritual Exercises of St. Ignatius (all which I have been trained in and serve as coach - mentor.) Only in pressing pause in my busy life can I have access to the treasures beyond measure - which lay waiting in this moment. What will I find? A deeper connection for sure, at least to what's inside of me. **Press Pause: " II" and Notice, then Re-connect.**

Pause. Ok. Got it. Now, connect to what? I'm going to be honest with you. When I practiced this exercise myself writing today I noticed, to my disappointment, that I was "under the weather." Ailments have spread across this state at epidemic levels and unfortunately, I could not avoid it. How do we talk about this inconvenient experience that happens to our bodies periodically? One thing getting sick does give us is a major "press Pause," and yet we have been taught to resent it. "When can I go on with my life," (as I know it) I might ask. And yet, the body is communicating something our mind can only scarcely grasp. One of my colleagues calls it, " a software upgrade." Ancient wisdom considers it part of the rhythm of life which affords us an opportunity to pause, and notice, and (gasp!) surrender. But not without a fight? It's very uncomfortable for us westerners especially if my life is run by my "to do" list. An imposition, at best, this is. Let's get it over with as soon as possible. In my case the ailment lasted three weeks, while others I know watched it progress to pneumonia after four weeks. Under the weather for sure! Not in control. Forced to pause day after day. Sigh. What do we connect with — and to — when our bodies undergo this process? And what about my "to do" list? This brings me to a a little story which had a big impact on me. Most of the early part of my life I ran from thing to thing, from task to task, and at night fell into my bed, exhausted yet relieved to be done. People who knew me teased me about about my written "to do" lists, scribbled on old letters, or Post-It notes, which I had on my desk or in hand, head down, going to my car. After a few years of this I noticed a pattern: If I accomplished my "to dos," I felt good about myself; conversely, if I didn't get it all done by the end of the day, I often felt discouraged. Deflated. Anxious. Pressured. Next morning I told myself, "I'll jump to it, and get it done." Literally, there was no time to take a pause, such as the kind I suggest above, much less to ask myself what I notice or am feeling. The pace of life thrust on me in school and college became the template for my career and home life. There was always one more thing to do. All important. How did I feel about it? You just do it (like the shoe advertisement). Right?!

When I look back I see that I was seeking a kind of approval in life - from somewhere - at least from authorities - now that I look back on it. What was approved of was: It's okay to take a "connect break" - when I go to church or see a friend or relationship. That WAS my connect break. If someone asked me how I was doing, I answered, "fine, okay" yet had no evidence to make that claim on other than if I completed my to do lists. Again, life for me was all about the externals and expectations. Life was so many demands I must submit to — for job, family, God and country. And Notre Dame! Pausing and checking in with myself seemed like a luxury — even for someone studying graduate level Psychology and Spirituality. How ironic is that? Even our psychologists and ministers / Priests are running around like chickens. Ah, such is the conditioning of this culture. Yet you would think we were impoverished and struggling to get our next meal or living in a shelter by the pace at which we live and work (some of us are and the pace may seem more relaxed but for the inner turmoil). The instinct of "fight or flight" emerges in all situations of stress — and it continues to rule — if unreflected upon. Sometimes in hindsight I wondered if my hurried responses to people asking how I was - "good, pretty good, fine, okay, well enough" - were not just expedient but also a way to deflect the fear that I was not worthy to be listened to more than a sound bite. What is most important in life easily gets confused in the world of the good-intentioned. It was to my surprise that someone from another culture (which is significantly less well off than most of us in the good ole' USA) taught me a lesson I will never forget. We were "working" on a volunteer project together one year in my 20's with passion and intensity, to help those who were suffering in our community. One day when I was all a flutter about my to-do lists — one for home and one list for the volunteer project - this person looked at me innocently and asked me how I was. I remember being taken aback, as this was not a convenient question at the moment. Then, I looked up, and she was peering into my eyes with head slightly bowed, quietly waiting as if she had all the time in the world. Sighing, I then answered, "I'm ok, just trying to get things done so I can relax later." She gently looked at me with concern and and pointed at my upper chest, "I'm not asking how you are 'doing,' I'm wanting to know, ***how is your heart***?" She said people in her village can tell when something is on the other's heart - especially some strong emotion. Her family taught her that we can't hide, even if we try. She commented that it's odd we think we can avoid others seeing what's really going on. The truth was I had lost my favorite family pet that week back in the midwest and another relative had been very ill. I missed them yet I had my life here. Honestly, I felt torn inside as I threw myself into my work and projects instead of facing the very real grief and loss. My face must have shown it.

She noted, **"Where I come from people want to know that — what's on another's heart. it comes first, before all else. Then the 'to-do' lists. We Connect, so we're not alone in this. (She had tear in her eye) Isn't THAT what gives life meaning?"** This exchange grounded me and I began to ponder on this question: who do I let in on how I am when I pause, and notice? Often its wise to be discerning. Now with a stranger we make an initial contact yet need time to see if its right and true to share more of our heart with them. So how do we get real? Admittedly, vulnerability is a risk, specially if we do not live in a small village where we are related to or know everyone on some level. This is the way many of our agricultural ancestors used to live until the 1800s. And the Third world. and convents. What changed? It's really about transportation bridging distances yet our communication often does not. And with the number of divorces and broken families we apparently could do with some more communication of what we notice inside. What is on our hearts? Yet if we are all connected on a device and not totally "there," how might we open the door to share what is really, truly going on, if even a snapshot? The lesson I garnered from that exchange made an indelible mark, especially since I experience myself as a heart-centered person. I guess we all are, according to her village's tradition. Yet clearly I can become instantly cut off — even from what's going on inside when in task mode. I wonder if others can tell that about us? Can our friends and loved ones tell whether we are in our hearts - or our head — more than we can?

PART 2: EXERCISES & GUIDED MEDITATIONS

Breathe. Press Pause. what do you notice?

When we join this with the first exercise of deep breathing it can look like this in the flow of our day:

EXERCISE I : *Press Pause ... and Breathe ...*

- at your doorstep before going in to office, or home, or another's place.

- Before turning on the car or stereo pause for a moment.

- Before making a call or text — stop, breathe.

- Before replying to email or social media, breathe first. pause.

- Increasingly my life at its rolling pace requires a tactile reminder to Pause so I ring a bell, or chimes. Then let it vibrate, before I return to a task.

- What if I come home and first thing, stand in silence looking at a picture or view, maybe even light a candle.

- What if I Pause, sit down for 15 seconds before diving into household responsibilities or engaging people there.

- Pause, by using these two eyes to look at the sun or a scene of nature's beauty.

- Before getting out of my car, I pause first.

- I Pause, before heading into a store (so I don't trip) with the list in one hand and cell phone in the other. I Breathe - I've got 5 seconds to spare.

EXERCISE II:

A. Inspired by that encounter this second Exercise or pivot point in this chapter goes like this:

What do you notice, when you pause, breathe, for a moment, and connect.

Look within. if you could put it in a word, a phrase, even an image ... what would it be?

Often in the past I would have been stumped or too tired to think of something. Thus, rather than fumble for an answer I have found a helpful image-making tool to notice my "inner weather." For me, individually and in a group, I find it much more helpful when someone else asks me the above question, rather than ask it of myself. It's like I am a proverbial "deer caught in the headlights," especially if I am with a person I admire or authority figure like a professor or boss or there is some other high stakes going on. Sometimes I just don't want to know. Do I really need to know right now? It was not until I was in a personal growth and development program that iI realized how important it is for me to know my inner weather, so to speak. Often I am so tuned into what is going on for others and the dynamics in the room that I'm literally distracted from my own interior. If my job depends on it then of course I will defer. Yet if its a habit in which I am really not paying attention to how to take care of myself in a balanced way, then burn out is not far off. I learned the hard way: Everyone loses in that deal — including those I serve. Gratefully, I discovered a tool to find out more of what's going on for me. In some circles it is known as a classic "icebreaker" for group introductions.

For oneself it can be a 1 minute tune in & tune up called, "a weather report."

No wifi required, no App needed from a weather channel, just a willingness to reflect on what's happening for me now, in my life. It's a connect to the Interior, with a playful twist. I use it with small process groups as a way to "check in." Why? It's a simple, noninvasive invitation to hear what people are bringing into the room as they meet listen, and speak. Especially if they might share from their hearts. As a facilitator this handy tool helps me get a pulse of the individuals in the group so that if someone seems "off" I know at least a little of the context as to why — without having to know the gory details (or one extreme case, whether someone's crisis might potentially derail or dominate group time.)

So shall we take a weather report of this present moment or the day so far?

B. THE INTERIOR WEATHER REPORT ...

Breathe. Press Pause. What is my current weather report in the interior of my country?

What do I notice as I look back on my day and even mentally look forward? If I could put that in an image which uses language descriptive of predictions by weather reports, what might that look like ?

Relax. You can Play with it, in your own words. Let your creative side express what is true in your life. You are freed from using details, only a brushstroke of what it's like on your insides.

Here are some examples I have heard:

I just come through a snow storm to get here.

It's looking partly sunny yet cold front coming in.

There a high pressure system looming.

Clouds overhead with a chance of evening showers.

Tornado watch for the upcoming weekend so battening down the hatches. Lightning and thunder on the work front and glad to be where its clearer. Big Clouds earlier opened up to bright sunshine and warm temps now.

Now come up with your own pithy statement which reflects what is really going on for you at this time. It's a gift you give yourself. That keeps on giving. It may be revolutionary for you and your family to express a little more than a one word response in valuable interaction.

QUESTIONS FOR REFLECTION:

Q.1 When people ask us, "How are you?" with what do you usually answer, and based on what information?

Q.2 It's curious that the Weather Channel is one of the most popular TV stations & Apps on the phone. Why might this be so?

Prediction of the future? Planning of our potential events? Preparation for our kids and family? What about the weather situation INSIDE of us, even of our family dynamic and its affect on others, not to mention ourselves.

Q.   3 What does it take to really find out the truth of what's happening in me, and what prevents me or distracts me from curiosity of finding out?

Q.4 Lastly, what is the cost if I don't pause periodically (even regularly) to find out what's coming through me?

APPLICATIONS:

1. What if we regularly did a Weather report with our family or our kids? How about at dinner time, rather than that awkward silence, we make it into a game! (aka Mary Poppins)

2. With our spouse or a colleague or a friend we haven't see in a while consider asking and sharing the weather report from the last week or month, even the brushstroke of the whole year.

3. What other application might you see in your life to pause & notice?

4. Jot down here some notes and consider when might these (or highlighted items in chapter) belong in your coming day / key relationships?

5. Consider wearing a shirt or button that says, "Pause. Take three deep breaths before you talk with me." :)

RECOMMENDED DAILY HYGIENE:

Just like: "Dentists recommend brushing your teeth twice a day, for two minutes, (I just saw this phrase on a billboard driving down Highway 99) what if we found out it's just as responsible to do the same for our internal systems status:

Press Pause, refresh, reset, restart, periodic internal

drive scan and assessment.

And apparently we ignore it at our own peril (Recent Studies show the correlation between unacknowledged stress and heart attacks, etc.)

SONG: Indian Canyon / Good medicine

Consider listening to the first song of the Tim Malone & Soul Fam cd as the chorus of this last phrase washes over you like a waterfall in the desert.

This original song came out of my own experience on retreat in the desert canyons outside of Palm Springs California. It is the first song on the "Tim Malone & Soul Fam" cd. The song is also found on iTunes, Amazon, and CDbaby, and other sites yet you can enter into the experience through a video online by clicking on this website below. The song is a story of my own pausing and participating in a healing journey through illness to wholeness. The tone is actually meditative and the visuals are mesmerizing. The lyrics: we can find Good medicine, right here, right when we find our inner indian canyon, May this song support you as you in finding your own style of Pausing & waking up to the treasures inside.

WWW.SOULFAM.ORG to Watch the Video

4: Being Still and Knowing

Portals to Refreshment,,,, any time of day:

Breathe.

(Press) Pause.

What do you Notice?

Be Still, and Know.

36

PART 1 - ORIGINS & INSPIRATIONS:

The next two chapters invite us deeper into this exploration of what we truly need to show up as a present human being, to ourselves and to others around us in refreshed and re-freshing ways. What does it take for me to be still and Know a deep refresh?

The following comes from a real life conversation overheard again and again in different contexts. A frustrated parent watches their active child bounce around the house playfully, with an abundance of energy. The parent has a reaction, maybe worried somehow and bursts out angrily: **"Can you be still for just two minutes?!"**

To turn the question around: Can we, as adults, be still for just two minutes? Without a prop — a screen, a book, drink, some entertainment, another's voice or a group / service leading us? When and where have you experienced this "just Being?" Savor the memory that arises. Write about this experience. **What if the scene above continued like this:**

The child, shocked into sitting position, looks up innocently to the parent and gulps, asking, head tilted,

"How about you? Can you be still for just ... two minutes... *with me ... ?" Or come out to play?* ;)

I would like to suggest that a habit of being still is countercultural. Growing up in the midwest united states in the 1960-70s in a religious family active in their parish and as moral upstanding citizens I learned to do. As first born of my entire extended family I excelled in doing. Doing "good" was praised — as a Boy Scout, as a Catholic youth, as neighbor and as member of many school organizations. At some point after a family member went through a long recovery I unconsciously took it that *my* role was to be a helper — like my caring family was in the community. To "do good" wherever I found myself was just what I tried to do. On the college campus, I became active as a chapel leader, an advocate for justice, an activist and pioneer on a student retreat team. From the Judeo-Christian tradition I understood the Ten Commandments and I took these very seriously — even to extremes at times — seeking perfection like the saints seem to attain as a sort of realistic goal.

Ironically, one of the commandments is to "keep the sabbath, to honor that day." In the tradition I grew up in this was translated as, "go to church on Sunday," and then followed by a delicious family lunch at a local restaurant. Then, family would drive back home to watch TV (football, etc.) and do homework or projects. That is pretty much what everyone seemed to do in this part of world regardless of religious tradition or not. Often, I would go into my room with wallpaper of trains and a poster that said, "Dream Big," and lay on my bed. Sometimes I would do just that — daydream - listening to the radio or favorite music album, alone, in solitude. Sometimes I felt connected, vaguely to a larger mystery out there, holding me. I savored these fleeting moments. However, often I was so focused on the future life ahead of me, and what I needed to DO to achieve that goal, that my mind was rarely still. Always there were competing thoughts and pressure. Before my eyes I entered visions of grandeur and above all, a place where I could rest my head, if only I might get there through more education, awards, & approval of the teachers. It was on the horizon, far enough ahead to keep me motivated through the many years of trudging day after day. So it seemed that something was driving me as well to achieve, yet later I realized the deeper mystery of life more often *invites* rather than prods or pushes me somewhere.

The thousands year old psalm I grew up with begins with: "Be Still and know I am the One ...with you through it all." Wow — what if the Source of life loved me no matter what I did or said. This would not even occur to me until my sophomore year at college away. That was a turning point, on a retreat far away from home, amidst a pivotal stage of choosing whether to continue in Pre-Med toward becoming a doctor or recognize that for whatever reason my grades were not what they were in high school. The more I studied the more I felt a kind of confusion about my path - not being quite what I'd imagined in that bed at home. I volunteered at a hospital bedsides and though I loved being present with the people I didn't feel comfortable there. Something wasn't quite right in the environment as if I were being nudged toward and bigger vision of healing and well being than alleviating physical symptoms. How was I supposed to know which way to go? I felt alone in the decision-making even though I am sure there were many authority voices to tell me what I should or should not do. Everyone cared, and for that I most grateful. When I asked thoughtful questions, though, most people weren't in touch with their own experience of how they got to where they were, or they just followed scripts laid out for them. My path seemed baffling to most of my loved ones. And of course, outside of the monastic tradition there wasn't really encouragement in the culture to truly pause and just be still in silence for periods of time. There were some refreshing guided retreats and events to reflect. Underlying it all we a clear focus so as to not get lost. As the old phrase went, "An idle mind is the devil's playground," or so we feared. Yet as I was later trained as a spiritual director to ask, "Where is the Source of life in all of this?" Years later I would see that to drive myself forward on that path to be a diagnostician MD any more would have not honored who I was, and was becoming. I had it right that my call was to the interior life, to be present to others in a healing way yet not under the skin literally — as doctors are trained to tend to — but the interior movements of a person's heart, mind, and soul. And not necessarily as a conventional priest / pastor of a parish or school, nor as a full time psychologist or professor. It was all so confusing in my 20s as what I am doing now wasn't even on the menu, you might say!

After my body gave out over the stress of those college years I was plunged into my own interior, not unlike what happened with many people watched their lives be transformed from within so as to be put on a renewed path of service in love. I began a new journey then, one that pointed directly to a balance of doing and being. For in being still, I would begin to know. Know what? Know a richness of life, like diving into the deep sea after living only on the shore. I would know depths and what lives there, a beautiful realm of human inner life, of intuition, how perceptions work, a myriad of feelings, of responses and reactions that make up a person's life. Yet more than that, I would be invited into the ocean of personal growth, and even transformation. What a wonder that we can experience life changing shifts— not just in changing our behaviors and habits (the field of psychology) but of opening to hearing something when we are still, in solitude, in silence with this body-being we call human. There, the monastics and contemplatives, the mystics and hermits, found treasures and wrote about them. I discovered a whole-ness in the tradition I was reared in that spoke to me like a ringing gong or a soothing bubbling stream: Be Still and know, listen, and a larger mystery in the universe speaks. And by being still, I might hear my own still small voice - in dialogue with something much bigger, even transcendent. I developed understanding, in fits and starts, through trial and error and through courageous exploration of what field to study and whether I was called to lifelong vocation as a religious. Not until my 30s, though, did I grow to develop the practice of being still and deeper inkling of knowing who and what is speaking within (and around me). Paying attention in the silence and stillness to what arises, and reflecting on this with other trusted guides led me to practice what is called, discernment. My 40s were a decade of honing these skills as a mentor with the Spiritual Exercises and a budding director of meditation retreats. Then responding to an invitation to guide young adults into their interior movements led into the dream of co-directing a Spirituality Center connected to Seattle University. In all of these discernments I received much clarity with help of a spiritual director who I met with monthly and have kept this supportive habit for the last twenty-five years. Being still as a means to knowing more who I am at the core, and who I am not took going into the deepest recesses of my mind, heart and soul. At the root of finding what is true and right for me, however, has been the practice of taking longer periods of being time, both daily and weekly. Thus, for over 15 years now I practiced this weekly, conscious habit: I learned to carve out four to eight hours each week of spending time just Being. It's a scheduled appointment on my phone calendar that I keep as sacred as any other meeting, including work. I creatively have found ways to build in moments during the week to apply the tools in this book. It is a life-saver. And continues to bear fruit beyond just the delight of spaciousness.

PART 2: EXERCISES & GUIDED MEDITATIONS

"BE STILL AND KNOW" GUIDED MEDITATION

I invite you to read these words out loud to yourself, slowly, in a
whisper and see where it leads you. What do you notice…

Be Still … and Know.

Be. Found…Here.

Be, … Still … Be, …. in the Silence.

Be . . . Here, Now.

Be . . .Home…in this moment. Be …

with what Is.

*Be Freed . . .from suffering… the constant
movement, responses, reaction.*

*Be released . . .from seeking, just for a
moment. (Breathe.)*

Let yourself be … found . . .as you are.

Be still and Know . . .you are found… In the Heart of Love.

Be Still…Be Found at home, At Last!

TAKING "DEEP MOMENTS:" Suggested ways to apply a "connect break" into our daily life:

What if you gave yourself a gift of a quiet moment each day. For example, schedule 2-5 minutes;

✓ to sit in your favorite chair, to pause, breathe and just Be. Relax into Still-ness, sink into the spaciousness this gives yourself. In this way, you get to take a connect break from the busy-ness of whatever holi-daze or future gaze, our mind wants to chew on. Re-Read this meditation aloud or silently, or consider recording your own voice so you can listen anytime, anyplace, like a storybook being read to you, comforting you. In this way we remember the best wisdom of the ancient deep moments and see why it was passed on a "must do" for so many of our did our ancestors .

✓ Commit weekly to a time of 1-3 hours, a half day of luxuriating in deep moments in solitude or sharing the delight with a loved one.

✓ In the above lives-style shift try "fasting" from electronics of any kind while Feasting on what else there is that is life-giving around you.

For the minutes or hours we courageously step out of the stream of the cultural spell consider these ways I have found essential to coming into the quiet peace:

✓ Begin by lighting a candle(s) to connect with light and our center. Place keys, phone, TV controller, etc. — and any intentions of what we want to let go of in a small box

✓ Ring a Bell or Gong (or alarm, if you must) to begin and end your deeper connecting time. Create a sacred space / kind of altar with photos, images, mementos to lead you into a time of true rest

✓ Open up a book of reflections or inspirations which leads you to your Inner Sanctuary (see below)

✓ Slower pace of walking around the house. Try walking meditation in or out. Bring a stick or binoculars to encounter nature out your front door.

✓   Center your attention on a favorite poem or meditative practice like the ones introduced in this Guide

✓   Play Musical instrument or favorite quiet background music / guided meditation CD

✓   In moments of solitude trust the silence can be your friend and a companion leading you to your beautiful inner self

✓   Acknowledge whatever sensations or emotions arise, however we might label them as *the* practice. Once attended to, this will grow you, like a garden, winter into spring, blooming. You, a Gift to the whole world.

Reflection Questions:

Q. What do you do when you are stressed and what what helps alleviate that for you?

Q. 2 Another way to ask this is what is the first thing you do when you get home from a day of activity, shopping, work?

Q. 3 What kind of habits might we choose in place of something which keeps us distracted (yet maybe agitated, restless) and instead leads us into this stillness or inner quiet?

SONG to rest in stillness and just being in a space of inner quiet:

"Slipping' into the Mystery" is number seven track on the cd Tim Malone and Soul Fam with these lyrics

I'm slipping into the ocean, slipping, into the sea, relax and we are held in the great mystery.

The Calling: A Poem from the Inner Sanctuary Within:

Drawn to go
In,
Not to go out. To stay, in Silent
moments sated.
HiBer-
Nate,
As it were.
Take
It
Slow-ly,
As one must,
When
Listening To a
Voice Speaking
Through
A clear-calling stellar Jay Alight upon the snowy
winter lawn:
Wake up.
Your sanctuary is here.

©Timothy Malone. (2002)

5: Listen, Heart Opens

Breathe.

(Press) Pause.

What do you Notice?

Be Still,

and Know.

Listen Now,

Your

Heart

Opens,

When Connecting ...

PART 1 - ORIGINS & INSPIRATIONS:

Now as a intentional "self-care practitioner" I have begun to listen, to truly listen. To really listen to what is around me and now more to what is within me, I need spaciousness. The poem foundation above gives permission to step out of the rushing stream of my life — if even for a few seconds or a minute - and get space. From there, coming back to the breath and taking quiet moments in between tasks throughout the day becomes a new habit. Once I have paused and allowed a minute of stillness I can begin to know something about what's happening for me right now. Waking up to the truth that I am not an automaton or an animal in reaction mode means I am now aware. I am gifted with being a human who has choices and options — and I'm aware of that once again. With this awareness I am in a position to consider new things. Using my five senses I can take in new information yet I can also access places within me that may have been ignored or blocked. Thus, truly I am poised to listen. Listen to what? In this chapter I offer ways to listen to what's going on — in my mind, my body, and even my heart's desires. There is a Chinese proverb that will aid us in our search for how to listen: The longest distance in the world is not from here to the other side of the Earth; ***The longest distance in the world is from the the head to the heart.*** Q. What does this phrase evoke for you?

Are there any experiences that come to mind when you hear this phrase? This toolbox invites us to remember, again and again, to listen & take care of the body and heart's needs. From this grounded place we can then respond - and act courageously - out of Love.

The tendency to jump to doing is understandable in these times: What can I do about it? What if the invitation lies in a subtlety rare as diamonds, and often misunderstood. Like the idiom, "the early bird gets the worm," the solution seems like it's first, to listen, then as soon as possible, do something about it. What if we look more closely at the birds around us in an attitude of curiosity to their actual behavior. Once the birds get up, do they work hard non-stop like our society in its emphasis on productivity before all else suggests? If not, how are we meant to live our lives?

Be Still, and listen from teachers in the animal kingdom. I have learned much from watching birds, especially their feeding and grooming habits. As I wrote above, "The early bird gets the word" was a common phrase at one time. What did this signify or try to engender in a student or young person? What does it mean and what do birds actually do when going for their meal?

Actually, if we pay attention to their feeding patterns, we might see something astonishing and instructive: Groups of Robins go into meadows in the morning and walk on the ground like hunters. They don't just dive into any old place in the turf. Looking closer one can see that they pause, be still, sometimes for several seconds while they cock their heads to listen. Apparently, when they hear the movement of the worm, or the buzzing of an insect, only then do they pinpoint the place and dig with all their focus down. Using the tool of their beaks, they can often pull up an entire elongated meal. What is happening here? From one perspective one can say they don't drum up their meal: The food is already there. It is with their patient trust, these birds use their developed senses and instincts, and find what has already been given in abundance. They show up, and are fully present to receive. Other animals such as owls, big cats, snakes, spiders all follow this same style of being still, waiting, listening and then simply acting in a way that involves receiving. Our world has been fashioned for us in a different way, however. Yet we can still learn much from these friends we share our habitat with yet are often oblivious of in our fast- paced movements. I have compassion for us humans who are still in fight or flight mode from previous generations who suffered much, and passed on the fear, "We will not have enough," though in reality we in the West live as so many kings and queens compared to anytime in history previous to us. And still we are quite anxious, and don't have time to be still for two minutes. What might we discover about what's inside if we Be still long enough? Maybe that's why we avoid it like the plague!

Be Still, and Know. Open up to hear what is the next step. Show up and listen. What if we get to receive something we need. Maybe we don't even have to knock ourselves out to get it. In my experience the listening function works best when I pair an earlier phrase, "what do you notice?" with this gem: "What do you *need in this moment*?" The first exercise is kind of personal CAT scan to ascertain the stress I am carrying in my body.

It's a portal into discovering what I need and a doorway to the deepest connection with this vehicle we walk around in. Yet sometimes its the basic needs which go unnoticed and cause quite an irritated state of being. For example, in almost a decade as a mental health counselor we encouraged our clients to a practice of checking in with ourselves about what we need in this moment. Honestly, I'm still honing the basic questions in the acronym H.AL.T: am I hungry,

47

angry, lonely or tired? What do I want to do then so I can be present and listen. When I'm uncomfortable and I don't know why give these next exercises a try.

PART 2: EXERCISES and GUIDED MEDITATIONS

Three avenues to listen and receive knowledge on the next indicated step to take:

1. LISTEN, LISTEN to the Body: A personal CAT scan to my inner stress

Breathe, Pause, and enter some stillness. Notice inner weather and when in some discomfort I allow my mind to relax and focus on this phrase as its primary task:

"I now listen to this body, to my heart as if it's the

most important person in my life."

I scan from my head to my toes like an X ray machine through the body. I pay attention to where the discomfort is arising from and breathe into that place for a few moments. If no particular area calls our attention consider a placing a hand on our heart or chest region and pausing for a few moments. We might even try crossing our two hands over our chest in a gesture of an opening heart that is willing to receive some tender loving care. Wherever we discover tightness or tension, be with this in a desire to be present with whatever is arising this moment. I ask: what might this sensation be trying to say to me right now? Is there an image this evokes for me?

To explore this more depth consider the classic focusing technique at www.focusing.org or even guided "mindfulness body scan" which I have pointed to clients from the San Diego Mindfulness institute or through www.plumvillage.org. If I am hearing nothing I may be dumbed and deadened to this still voice within so I find it helpful to pay attention by means of some prompts in the exercise below.

2. THE H.A.L.T. EXERCISE :

10 SECOND PROMPTS for the daily journey of self-care and opening our capacity to be present to another. H.A.L.T. is another way to pause, notice and listen then ask what do I really need right now? If I find I'm really stressed or somehow feeling, "out of it," and not able to identify what I'm feeling I do myself (and others) a favor and ask:

AM I HUNGRY,

ANGRY,

LONELY,

OR TIRED ?

OR ALL FOUR?

H — HUNGRY

This one may seem simple: if Hungry, then what shall I do next?

Suggestions:

A. Eat something, preferably substantial — a fruit or real food to supplement your intake until your next regular meal.

Or if I'm past my regular meal time, I know other reason why my body is speaking may be loudly!

B. If not hungry for food then hungry for what?

If its not about food then might I be Hungry for something else, less solid, like: attention, affirmation , validation, approval, or some other valid need?

Take a moment to consider what this might be, to become aware of then you can choose or go down this list to see what else might be going on.

A - AAAH, Agitated, Annoyed, even Angry (or just plain frustrated?)

Or whatever strong emotions coming up in this form: Anxiety / Nervous or kind of Afraid?

Sad, Disappointed, Down or Blue?

Whatever the emotion, I have discovered its essentially neutral - it's just natural energy from the body trying to communicate with you to get your attention.

It may have been bottled up for a long time. You may be grieving a loss. Any of this resonate with your experience in this moment?

Suggestions:

A. Consider an internal Check-in with a WEATHER REPORT. See if an image helps you name it.

Then pay attention to see if any situation or person's face arises. Listen.

THE KEY: Let it be acknowledged and let out into the light.

Once it is named and honored as having a right to be there, in my humble experience some communication with a trusted friend or comrade may get to root of what we are stirred up about.

Next: Counselors and Therapists have encouraged me to next get it out of my body. Somehow by moving the energy we can direct it like superheroes as its fuel for your day, meeting, or project or facing a conflict in our lives.

How might you effectively release or direct it?

My experience so far shows that one or any combination of these practices does the trick: speak it out, take a brisk walk, engage in Exercise or play sports which allow me to make contact with a surface or ball. In a safe and private space, I whack with a tennis racket or hit pillows on a couch, yell in my car or into a towel or pillow. Sometimes just twisting a towel with all my might and groaning does the trick!

(disclaimer: any of this is best practiced under support of a certified coach, counselor or therapist to be safe and sound!)

L — Lonely

Q. When i'm feeling lonely I would most like to _____ ?

Suggestions from my on how I find some balance in my life living with the tension of being social and be in aloneness:

Reach out - speak to someone in the office or neighbor nearby. Make a phone call. Write a letter or text

For true solace, contact a person who you have a real, heartfelt connection with If you have a pet, this may soothe or comfort.

Lonely: The word literally means, "I am Longing, for a connection or go to a place of home, in some way.

T — Tired in other words, **are you feeling sleepy, yawning, low energy, fatigue, exhausted**? If not, have you had a *healthy* regular meal today or if down. Or if you're down, in a funk then go to H or A again to check if this resonates. If not then here are some ... **Suggestions from a recovering workaholic:**

If, in your car, pull over somewhere and then proceed to next step. I you only got a minute or two? Start by wisely setting your alarm, for one to ten minutes wherever you are, whatever your can manage once you discover you're very tired: Close your eyes, breathe, rest for a moment by counting down from three to one then say, "Relaxing... at ease ... calm."
Ideally, take a 10-20 minute nap somewhere where you will not be disturbed. Even putting the seat back in the car I have found that 20-40 minute naps are most restorative..

P - A pp bathroom break
Some Practical additions to the above include the letter P. I love how in the the airplane attendants say, "in the event of an emergency, put on your mask first, before assisting others." I liken these refreshment tools to that wise advice with the oxygen mask and realize one of the letter missing might be just plain basic need to go to the bathroom. Asking myself when agitated: Do I need to go pp? We can gently check in and ask ourselves this before we drive or go into a meeting. How is it to converse with another or be present when we need to go? Might that be why you're feeling oddly restless or fidgety ? :)

G — Ground:

Do I need grounding, centering? Like a live wire that needs to ground in order to focus the electricity as it sparks so are we after being wound up. What grounding practices do I find helpful in these situations. Certainly practices above and connected to a loved one assist me. In this case we are going to suggest switching the phrase: "Don't just sit there, do something ..." to " Don't just do something, sit here!"

O — Open and orient my heart and mind.

When I am overly in my head - analyzing, judging, critical or complaining — I know something needs rebalancing.

It may be I just need a reminder to Open & Orient Heart to be my best self, and to be of benefit in this situation before me?

The is when I most need to Open door to CONTACT & CONNECT to my higher, deeper "true" self or to higher, bigger power. Then ask myself I how can be of service to someone or some cause bigger than me, especially to people who are in real need of the basics in life. When I lift my head long enough I might see persons on the street begging or suffering. Then I might offer some food or give a stranger a smile with a hello.

Q. what other way of offering service or benefit in our village community helps you open your heart and mind?

Okay now it's time to add your own additions and letters that you notice work for you in your daily life!

3. ACTIVE LISTENING WITH ANOTHER:

This is truly the gift that keeps on giving. Simply, this exercise involves another person in your life who we want to communicate with or listen to. This is especially useful if you find yourself struggling to really hear them. Or they tell you that's what they experience from us you as as listener. So, first take care of your own needs before engaging the other by checking in on the exercises above.

Once you can be totally present in this way you are ready and available to listen this these suggested conditions:

✓ Arrange so there will be no interruptions

✓ Silence cell phones

✓ Sit or walk in a private space

✓ With agreed upon time parameters.

52

✓ When I do this exercise with groups, I suggest 5 minutes for each person, then rotate, with 5 minutes to share about the experience of listening / speaking together at the end.

Essentially, we listen without comment for 5 minutes. We maintain eye contact, and express in our body language or words saying something like, " I'm interested in what you have to say. You are important and valued." I find it helpful to start with a focusing question, like:

How was your day? (work, meeting, trip, etc.)

Share your weather report, with anything you would most like me to know or "What's on your mind,, or heart that you want to share with me at this time?"

If this is not in your repertoire then consider try practicing this with a close friend or spouse, even a family member. Feedback from one couple at a workshop I led included: "I discovered new things about the other person I had known for twenty years" - and "I didn't know how hard it was to keep quiet for 5 minutes and not jump in !"

Active Listening is a skill which can be learned in workshops and trainings worldwide.

Reflection Questions:

1. What I notice with these exercises is a reflexive opening: When I am present to myself, its body and its needs, I can truly be more present to others. Listen Now, Your heart opens. When have you had an experience of something like this?

2. In your experience what helps you to open your heart and no close it - to others (even to our own body / heart?)

3. The active way to consider all this is: how might I love myself today?

4. In this climate of divisiveness and acrimonious talk from many news sources it's natural to get frustrated, discouraged, disheartened and even downright angry at the chaos and injustices I see around me. Yet how do I both listen as well take care of myself, not taking in what is toxic ?

5. How might I put my values in action from a grounded, centered place of listening discernment, of responding rather than of reaction? Who might be a companion to support me in this quest to live with my heart open to discover what is mine to do?

<u>SONG</u> — I Love myself today

The story from my life learning of how to love myself was made into a song number three on the Tim Malone & Soul Fam, entitled, "I love myself today ..."

Chapter Five & Three-Quarters: Modern Stress = Dis-Connection

AN INTERMISSION

CONNECTING TO …

HUMOR and COMEDY

as

REFRESHMENT

PART 1 - ORIGINS & INSPIRATIONS:

Imagine we are in London at Kings cross station entering the portal at platform five and three quarters. Ready, set, go and rush on into a wall - that opens us up into another world! That world looks like this: How about we Take a break now from the courageous effort of trying to shift habits so ingrained in us as we trust progress is happening toward more moments of showing up as our best self! So it's time to do whatever we want with no heed to the cost ... just do it! And below is just the Self-Help book for the task. Here it goes: My next book is already on the cutting floor and so now I am introducing to you this Future NY times best seller due out just in time for Christmas / Easter rush! This True to life (and sometimes hilarious) book compliments the book you are reading. It is the mirror alter-ego what we have been engaging so far in that the thesis is: *"Get refreshed - who has time for that?! It's so much easier to get distracted, now* yet we may need some added extra guidance as to, "how ..."

So, Here it is ... boldly entitled: **Get stressed NOW:**

PART 2: EXERCISES & GUIDED MEDITATIONS

Get stressed now: *10 tried & true ways to stay stressed, tight, wound up and delicately poised for an early exit..."* Here is a "Big Gulp" of the highlights just bursting out of the table of contents:

1. Life is a race, so get to it – it goes to the winner, that is, the fastest, the richest (and the nastiest)

2. You can always have more, so go out and get more ... NOW! Remember: the worm goes to the early bird!

3. It's all about achievement so reflect on this: what have you proven today and done today that's impressive and measurable?

4. Make your mark on the world now, stop wasting your time, before it's too late and we're wheelchair-bound...

5. Screens are the answer, the *real* medicine of our age, so go spend as much time in front of a screen as humanly possible. You'll never regret as it's safe & FDA approved!

6. Acquiring more information will make you happy. So, anytime you have a question or want to find something out, go on the Internet now! Don't wait until later. Time is of the essence! (See how impressed your friends and business associates will be at the next event when you pull out all YOU know!)

7. Follow every impulse to its full and natural conclusion, and don't forget about the next great beer or entertainment that EVERYBODY is raving about! Buy, collect, and gather everything you are interested in that moment - don't let a moment go by.

8. It's not about love – your wife or family wants things, toys, machines, the latest and greatest models of everything so buy it now - or you'll miss out and be one step behind your office mate, or neighbor, and end up feeling like a Loser …"love" – its about stuff: our spouse / pet & / or family wants things, you know, toys, machines, in fact, the latest and greatest models of everything… so buy it now - or you'll miss out & be one step behind your office mate, or neighbor, & end up feeling like a Loser. (not recommended) …

9. Sabbath means go to church or temple to get God's blessing on your prosperity and expanding property and influence. In the pew, use the time to scheme and strategize your future of acquisitions.

10. Lastly, we all do well to remember Stress is just an illusion – the word wasn't even used the way we do now until 100 years ago. Whatever …

11. The point of all of this? We all need to be on constant vigilance and on emergency alert 16-22 hours a day just like the Coast Guard and NSA.

12. Just in case and immediately after reading this join any three letter organization that most gives you real security such as _____ .

Reflection Question:

Please fill in the blank above and as your deep reflection and connection exercise during your writing, keep thinking of all the things we are entitled to. Then make a number of to-do lists for tomorrow to Get, get, get because the pursuit of happiness has gotta feel like this overdrive heart pulsing intensity and a felt sense of grand control over my destiny.

SONG: "Standing: Got the Blues" on the cd — or the Roar of "Kitty Tiger Joy Joy."

And now after all of that funny business here is what you have all been waiting for …

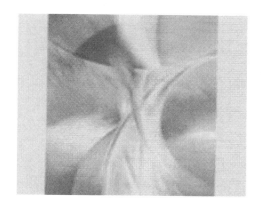

6: Connecting to a Heart of Gratitude

Breathe. Pause.

Notice.

Be Still and Know.

Listen, Heart

Opens,

When

Connecting to

Abundant YES.

PART 1 - ORIGINS & INSPIRATIONS:

When I traveled on pilgrimage for one year solo journey the only screens were desk top computers and the internet was new and found only in bigger towns. I found great comfort in starting my day with breakfast of champions: porridge and a quote from a former UN secretary from before I was born that called us to be grateful for what we have now and to look forward with an attitude of "yes" to that which will come. (Dag Hammarskjöld). Upon return to the states just before 9-11 a practiced an adapted version of this and used it with groups and individuals that I led to visits of house of worship to build bridges of understanding during that shell-shocking time. Since then screens have abounded to the point where most people have multiple devices in their bedrooms, much less houses. Only recently the insight came to me that the reason I spend so much time in front of a screen arises from the need for comfort and soothing. Like so many of us these days we are dependent on this tool for self-soothing which at its best takes me out of my worrying mind. The other side, of course, is that there is never enough comfort to be found in my life - to soothe life's bruising past and present - and this make it very difficult to be grateful for what I have. I now understand more of my own inner workings which are really primal instincts to be around a fire, warm, comfy and held in the gaze of someone or something that approximates nurturing. How many of my desires and hopes in life revolved around securing more comfort and images of my being secure. In compassion for all of us how many of our motivations to get more and better, new and improved, come out of this longing to be filled and fulfilled. This may not be news to some of you yet for me it struck like lightning with a tenderness of seeing a child reach for comfort when it needs it now. It's quite a leap of faith to say, "No, I don't need that. I am thankful for what I have. It's enough. I am enough as things are."

There are so many books and practices out there on the benefits of being grateful and giving thanks, sincerely, from out hearts. Take a look at any spiritual wisdom tradition's writings and we can see a theme of recommending thankfulness as a meditation. Why does it require something outside of us to remind us to celebrate thanksgiving more than we do? Ah, this has eluded me for years. Now I know through experience that the act of gratitude calls upon my higher self to intervene in what the mind habitually gnaws upon - worrying about the past or anxiety about the future. Gratitude is a practice which takes me into the present. This is like a loving parent calling the young one to focus right here. It is redirecting our attention. As adults we can either give that over to someone or something around us — spouse, boss, minister, an expert or a machine — or we can begin to redirect ourselves toward daily positive outlook on our life forward. I know for myself it was from outside that I learned of the importance of gratitude practice. There are too many people to mention here yet it really hit home during a personal challenge in my life that without a daily naming of what I am grateful for I get lost in the jungle of the mind by the end of the day. Thus, now daily for almost eight years I name at least 5 things / people / situations I am thankful for and I fall to sleep like a contented little baby who knows he has everything he needs.

PART 2: EXERCISES and GUIDED MEDITATIONS

Four gratitude practices to refresh us for the life flowing in and out of lives marked at times by loneliness and contentment. All of these work in one to five minutes and which I have found particularly helpful at one time or another:

1. <u>Gratefulness grounding Guided Meditation for the morning</u>

Or any other times in the day in which I lose my center and grounding. Much of these exercises I need to practice in morning and throughout the day when I lose my anchor. There are many books and research exhibits how the brain literally changes chemistry when we practice gratitude so try it out for size and see how if you notice a shift in mood or outlook.

Here is a Gentle Reprise of our previous guided meditations with ancient ways of opening heart to Gratitude:

I draw in three slow, deep Breaths. I Pause. Come into some Stillness.

As my Heart opens I remember this simple truth:

I am grateful to be alive at this time.

I have this day before me.

With this next breath

I come into the present moment. With the next inbreath,

I notice what I already have, now, in my life, and that it

is a gift. Feeling life come through my nostrils I come

back to my center.

I connect to my desire to be grateful (even if there is resistance to go there).

Allowing whatever arises just to be, I gently ask myself:

What is one thing I am particularly thankful for at this time _____? Savor this which

you have named for a few moments, consider writing it down in a journal or drawing an

image.

2. <u>ONE MINUTE to an Attitude of Gratitude</u>

Write down five things for which I am grateful:

_____

The KEY: Without thinking too much about it, just start writing stream of consciousness. For Example, bring to mind the people and things that are a blessing, a gift in my life right now. Consider also gratefulness for who I AM —In this vein name some Positive qualities I see in myself (or that others have commented on). Third, what are some foundational assets I have in my life right now? *Lastly, if you have time, consider this next step for purpose of integrating and connection to others:* Name these people, places, things and qualities about yourself that are admirable out loud.

Take a moment to savor these like taking in the scent of a rose or a gorgeous sunset.

3. AN ORIGINAL MANTRA OF THANKFULNESS FOR DAILY REFRESHING THE MIND & HEART:

The Short Version

"For the Abundance Received . . . I Give Thanks.

For the Abundance to Come, Trusting it will Come,

... I say, "YES!!"

The Full Version with the hand movements - Abundance expressed: As you

breathe in,

Cup your hands in front of you like a bowl and bring

those cupped hands up into your heart slowly as you

say these words

"For the Abundance Received . . ."

As you breathe out take a moment to reflect on and cup into your heart the gifts of people, events,

encounters, synchronicities

that have come into your life today and say:

" I Give Thanks."

At your heart bring your hands together with thumbs resting on the chest and fingers together

facing upward then bow slightly.

Was you breathe in again form your hands in a bowl shape again and slowly extend your arms

into a receiving position as you speak these words:

"And For the Abundance to Come,"

Stretch your arms out to full length in front of you, opening your hands wide and to either side,

saying:

" Trusting it WILL Come ..."

As you breathe out raise your hands high, palms up to accept with confidence the gifts to come

- your eyes looking skyward:

"I say, "YES!!"

APPLICATIONS IN DAILY LIFE:

Write your own gratitude phrase by using words which resonate with you:
For example, I insert a word that is "current" for me in place of the word "ABUNDANCE"
above:
"For that which has been received _____, (name the gift received) I give much thanks,"
"and for that which is to come, trusting it will come, I say, _____ "

This gratitude phrase can last ten seconds -- or three minutes, depending on your willingness to read it slowly - or use it as a kind of stretch or Yoga meditation.

Also, this can be spoken or can be silent, or made with gusto, especially at the end; saying "YES" -- with a full assent to trusting your own unfolding life amid the mysteries of the universe as it renews each year the Earth into Springtime -- which is, of course, is no small thing.

A Daily Meditation of our Consciousness

As former Co-Director of the Ignatian Spirituality Center in Seattle and 15 years retreat director with the Spiritual Exercises this is my version of the five-step Daily Examen that St. Ignatius practiced 500 years ago (in a Spain which reached heights of glory not unlike our own.)

1. Become aware of your higher, deeper self / transcendent presence.

2. Review the day with the lens of gratitude and openness.

3. Pay attention to your emotions / interior movements as you watch the DVD of your day play out from your rising to bedtime (up to this moment in the day)

4. Choose one feature of the day and ponder it thoughtfully with an eye to seeing what was life-giving and might have been life-draining.

5. Consider this in light of discernment of what belongs in your life.

Look toward tomorrow with eye to receive & offer Love in Service to others.

Reflection Questions:

1.   When might one of these exercises of naming the things you are thankful for or reviewing our day best fit into your daily routine?

2.   If we choose morning, at meals, or before bed, for example, when might you creatively place this into your schedule and what tools or people can support you in this new habit?

3.   Who might you invite to you join in on moments of expressing gratitude? Where and what medium / activity suits you at this time?

SONG: MUSIC TO ENHANCE YOUR EXPERIENCE:

Invite you to enjoy the ORIGINAL SONG — *"Come back to the Valley"* from the Tim Malone & SOUL FAM CD as an image of refreshment and gratitude experienced in an adventurous way as inspired by my seminars on J RR Tolkien's writings as soulful.

7:   Connecting to Our Nature

Open Eyes and Heart

I Find my deeper Connection

to My Home in Nature:

If you truly love nature, you will find beauty everywhere.

- Vincent Van Gogh, credited with founding modern painting

PART 1 - ORIGINS & INSPIRATIONS:

Almost every day I go outside and commune with nature. If even for a few minutes beside my car before I launch into my day, I bathe in the colors of life around me - trees & bushes, the shades of green, flowers and mushrooms, weather in the sky. I take in the symphony of bird songs and of wind or rain rustling the leaves in due season. Sometimes I take my shoes off and luxuriate in the feeling of my toes in the soft, lush grass, a kind of "earthing" on holy ground. It wasn't always a priority for me to stop, look around and take it in. In fact, while living in a city in the grandeur of the Northwest many of us look to the weekends to get out and hike after a drive of forty to sixty-minutes drive away. Now I am learning that there is beauty everywhere, if I have but the eyes to see and patience to pay attention just a little longer, even the city has secret pockets of beauty.

When my life slowed down I opened more to heart-opening nature viewing opportunities for a real connection that refreshes mind, body and soul. In this postindustrial age where we can literally live inside a building or vehicle 24 hours a day, researchers have been observing the impact on humans. In Europe doctors are treating a condition that has been recently named, "nature deficit disorder." The antidote? Nature Therapy. A doctor gives a prescription to a miner or an engineer to go to the Black Forest to restore. In Tokyo the Japanese urbanites are retreating from the skyscrapers and factories on weekends for what they are calling, "Forest Bathing." In fact, the deficit has been recognized like a warning beacon that draws them into ancient places (often forgotten in modern day) such as the wooded Shinto temples & rustic hot springs in the country. People are waking up to the reality that being "plugged in" all the time has its limitations.

Billboards in the Puget sound (paid for by National Educational Ad agency) depict two panels: the first is a boy on his Nintendo handheld console playing a video game, eyes wide with intensity. The second panel proceeds to show the same boy near a stream with a live frog in his hand, this time eyes wide in awe and wonder, maybe even simple joy. The only words across the 15 foot screen are "unPlug." In an attempt to reach people of color in the more industrial urban areas the state park departments at "Discover the Forest.org" now has massive billboards as a reality check for parents to redirect their children to put down the bright screens and plug into what is alive. And then there is the entrepreneurial side of capitalism that trickles down to those who will train and certify you to become a "forest bathing" coach or guide. The need is great and yet how might we find it right in our back yard or nearby park, through a window or up close?

Below are a few of the ways I have found particularly helpful to Unplug, and get refreshed in nature, sometimes in a few short minutes. Before work, on a break, after a long day, really in any season, these strategies can serve us. And in my experience there are permanent, positive effects to our whole Being. Come back to the Valley, the earth below our feet.

PART 2: EXERCISES and GUIDED MEDITATIONS

The First Exercise:

Connecting to my essential nature from wherever I am :

Stand in the place where I am. As a way to locate myself look up, then look down.

I Refresh, first, with the 3 deep Breaths. Pause. What do I Notice, around me? Being Still

for just a moment, I Know more as I Listen.

With my eyes closed for a second, I now consciously allow my Heart to open by

visualizing my favorite flower to bloom or scene from nature:

I Connect To Gratitude,

For just simply being in Nature,

Being of Nature,

Being Part of Nature.

I Connect To Ancestors, who have come before me on this land & to my family who walked

many paths on the earth.

I Connect to the Source of Love, I allow my Creative Energy to flow, sensing my Body

awakening with the next Breath taken from my toes to my nose,

I get to emerge more refreshed, since I have Come Home to myself, today,

everyday, every week, every season of my rich life!

<u>The Second Exercise:</u>

From indoors we still get to connect with the Natural World by trying a new kind of screen. Let's Unplug, for one minute and all you need is a window. Even at work we get to make contact and find our deeper connection to the Natural World, through the brilliance of your five senses. Surprisingly versatile, the first step of this exercise can be engaged for one to two minutes at work, or home, in a hospital room or waiting in line — anywhere with a window into nature - be the street or parking lot trees or a green space.

<u>Unplug</u> <u>to Connect:</u>

I begin by stopping whatever I am doing or holding and consciously looking out a window.

I open my hands to receive. I take a deep breath,

paying attention to whatever is on *this* screen, before me.

If the Sun is streaming in on some part of you,

close your eyes, feel the sun's rays on your skin, and savor for a few moments.

With or without the presence of the Sun, allow your eyes to pan the view and name what you see,

interiorly, as if seeing it for the first time - Apprehend the sky, the trees, the ground, the light

dappling, or clouds in their parade of movement.

With your next breath, take in the unfolding scene, like a movie or Monet painting. Spread your arms out before you and cup in all you see, taking it into your heart. you get to take it ALL with

you fro the rest of the day.

(Look deeply, drink it up, like a latte!)

<u>The Third Exercise:</u>   <u>Refresh by bathing in Nature</u>

If you have some more time the previous Nature Exercise can be expanded by going outside on your break time: This fuller version is 3-5 minutes in that it blooms from an action in which you take a conscious "break," that is, step outside (for a smoke break - even if you don't).

Sometimes I call it a "sun" break - or a "press pause button break." If you are on a timed break, I suggest you remember to set your phone alarm & put it back in your pocket or purse.

Begin with the Unplug and Connect meditation above as your foundation for this exercise. Next step is to find a spot next to something alive where you won't be disturbed. Then you get to check in with all five of your senses, (consider one sense for each of your five fingers), one at a time:

1. What do you see, that is alive, moving or growing. Take it in, savor sky or tree, landscape or architecture ?

2. What do you smell around you or on the breeze coming from nature?

3. What do you feel — on your skin, face, nose or exposed skin?

4. Touch something that comes from nature — a leaf, tree bark, a leaf or acorn on the ground, for example. What is the texture to your fingers?

5. What do you hear? Feel free to close your eyes in order to take in the sound with added clarity. Beyond the machines or industry what can you pick up that is emanating from the natural world. Savor it like Sound Healing from a musical instrument.

The Fourth Exercise in two parts:

Communing with nature we may find that *touching Nature nurtures.* A. Communing with Life - a tree - and the ground of Earth:

> Find a nearby tree, especially one you appreciate in some way.

> Simply place your hand on the tree in some place.

> Keep your finger or hand there for at least thirty seconds. Notice the texture.

> Feel the bark or leaves, the branch or sap, the flower, fruit or moss.

> If you like to walk in your neighborhood or a park, considering touching various trees on your path gently for a few moments.

B. Touching Ground

A one minute contact with the ground: now called by some, "earth-ing." First, check for a safe area to step on in bare feet or socks. Slowly take your socks or shoes off — while maintaining calm balance. Place your tender feet on the surface — preferably on soft grass — or a sandy beach. As you breathe in, close your eyes and tune into the sensation of the nerve endings on the soles of your feet and toes, your skin to the earth. Enjoy the sensations. Breathe in from deep in the earth whatever it has for you, its beloved progeny.

The Fifth Exercise: A date with nature

Dare yourself this week to go on a nature "date" by visiting a local park nearby for at least ten minutes.

When many of us were children in school this was termed or coined, a "field trip," though usually it was to a museum or a place which enacted the "pioneer days." The best of intentions was for us to get out and unplug from our routines. In school rarely did we "just" go to a park as entertainment or educational, yet these resources now can certainly be both. Even more, this "nature date" can be a key aspect of how we practice "deep Moments" from chapter four or where we try out the exercises in this book in an undisturbed setting.

A Nature date as a Pilgrimage to a National or state park:

I live near one of tallest volcanic mountains in the country, called Mount Rainier. This and most other National Parks are really pilgrimages to the Pristine and Primordial.

Each summer I plan for 3-5 times to visit, camp or serve as volunteer at one of three natural treasures within a three hour drive. A State parks pass also opens up hundreds of destinations to do everything from picnic while on a road trip (rather than an indoor restaurant) to recreation opportunities galore for kids and adults alike. If the lens of our mind is shifted a bit by broadening our definition of a "park" to visiting a realm of mysteries which have their own scared life to respect and honor then we are leaning from recreational tourist into the realm of a pilgrimage. Once on this wavelength we have access to an infinite number of experiences even if we visit the same areas twice. Where is the closest state or national park for you?

When might you consider a trip — or a pilgrimage in the next season?

Taking deep moments and sabbaticals to consciously set out on a Pilgrimage into natural wonderlands.

For me, the fruit of opening up and listening in stillness has been the realization that it's a self-care practice for me to plan a sabbatical every seven years - whether it's paid for my an institution or out of my own pocket.

Not unlike professors at the university and religious life there is a kind of healthy break and shift toward time for creative expression every six to seven years.

A pilgrimage involving spending time in unspoiled natural areas not only refreshes you but it resets you for a re-newed purpose, perspective (and sometimes, a new mission) and provides an environment for a creative project to receive new inspiration toward refreshed completion.

REFLECTION QUESTIONS:

After each exercise, write in a word or a phrase about what you are taking away from your experience, whether it was 1 minute or 15.

Consider journaling to expand your sense of what was happening inside you as you encountered Nature on its own terms.

1. When I tried one of these exercises, what struck a chord with me was _____ Something that

resonated with me or I discovered was _____.

73

Something that surprised me _____ or disturbed me _____ .

2. What would it look like to make a habit of this, taking myself - and maybe with family?

3. What happens to us if we don't spend time in nature — or acknowledge its existence?

What happens to our perceptions of the world, to our vision of the future, to the least among us, to our culture?

4. How might you participate in the restoring of balance in our culture with nature and industrial

side by side? for example, look at photo of nature or wild animal, that you took, or from

another source such as going to park or zoo or aquarium. What does it evoke in your to return

to that place internally ?

SONG :

You are invited to listen to the original song from the cd which perfectly companions this chapter, titled — *Find yourself in Nature." it is a stream of consciousness meditation while sitting in a backyard meadow watching life abound on a summer day. Or what other favorite song or symphony inspires your finding a deeper connection to your essential nature, your relationship to your habitat and your interdependence with it all?

8: Connecting to the Source and Creating a Sustainable Lifestyle

I Connect now to the Sustaining Source of my life.

Where I Find Creative Soulful support,

I Come Home to myself

and Become a Loving, mindful presence in the universe.

PART 1 - ORIGINS & INSPIRATIONS:

The Quest to continue connecting to the sustaining soulful source of support throughout our lives.

After my physical limitations were faced and I experienced a breakthrough in realizing I needed to spend more time being still, a whole new world of exploration opened up for me. In 1993 I began meditating daily and the years passed such that I could not imagine a day without touching the silent stillness, even now. Early during those last 25 years when I imagined taking vacations it wasn't to a tropical place but a draw to spend time on retreat at monasteries in Europe and later in Asia. As I look back on that period what emerges is watching a man on a curious quest to try on a variety of meditations styles as a way to connect more deeply to my new life unfolding. This search involved training with monks and nun teachers who dedicated themselves to stewarding the silence, you might say. What is more, they viewed themselves always as beginners rather than experts, as simple human beings who welcomed me alongside in their exploration to the core of the heart crowded in this over-mechanized culture. Invariably, even as these men & women I have been blessed to practice with got in their later years, (such as Thich Nhat Hanh (Thay), the Dalai Lama, Desmond Tutu, Richard Rohr, Thomas Keating, William Johnston SJ) the more they wisely talked about the need to begin listening to what the body, emotions and deeper being are saying to us: Clues they have for our becoming fully human and fully alive. On retreats with them and their monasteries I took note and grew in understanding. In time when I began to facilitate retreats it was clear that I still had more deepening and integration ahead -- to descend from my head in its intellectual musings to my heart with its own intuitive language. The funny thing about it is that later teachers would come out of daily life in forms unexpected. "When the student is ready the teacher shows up," the ancient sages often say. Each day now the monastery is here with its moment by moment opportunities to practice.

There is a point in personal development, however, when the inner guru shows up and gently asserts: There is a world beyond what teachers and external input with all its helps can take you. There are many tools out there and they are not all right for me all the time. How could I possibly do them all each day? A major wake up for me came as I grew in confidence and autonomy: I get to decide which ones take me home to be embodied in the life I have chosen today. No one can motivate me when it comes to my daily life - unless I live in a monastery as a monk and I give them the power to structure my life in a sort of symbiosis. I have chosen a different path which doesn't have built in external support. And there is much freedom in this while living in the tensions of a countercultural life. Yet the fruit is the art of making a life, a pioneering task: I get to keep planting my garden year after year with inner guidance and see what blooms. Sometimes we co-create this with another. This requires lots of support and a periodic review so inertia doesn't just lead me into the ditch again; Care giving as entangled again in co-dependent behaviors. Thus, every so many years I am faced with discerning which practices fit, and the where and when - - and to release the ones that no longer serve me - or others who may rely on me in some way. Then there is the question of once planted in my life how might I keep these helpful renewed practices at the forefront rather than letting them drop to the back burner when the next challenge or big project swamps our budding efforts.

For me there came a time in which I had to build a suitable lifestyle of health and wellbeing as burnout was imminent again. This meant asking what is essential and creating a daily, weekly, monthly and annual rhythm which sustains the pouring out of my life in service to others. In some circles this is called "a Rule of Life," and in others, its just plain sustainability. So that you get a sense of what this means practically I would like to share with you the rhythm of activities and practitioners which anchors me day in and day out. Simple, cost free and sustaining support that has always been available combines with my accessing the services of low cost skillful practitioners into a financially realistic lifestyle. By almost eliminating the need for coffee and alcohol I save enough money each year for a vacation anywhere in the world. The wonderful thing about committing to put these in my life is that when I practice them I don't need what culture says I need to cope in a distracted, consumerist way: The TV, overeating and shopping as coping strategies fall more into weekly than daily occurrences! Below is less a list and more of a way of life. By integrating all the experiences and best practices shared in previous chapters my life has come together into an integrated whole — yet from within rather than an outside authority telling me what I should do. I ask for support on a regular basis to keep self-care and sanity as a rule and not the exception.

Thus, my current life is a testimony the power of regular ritual and soulful habits to ground and transform a simple life into an extraordinarily fulfilling adventure.

DAILY

The morning 3 breaths, meditation, practices in above chapters including bedtime gratitude list

I connect with the source in nature sometime in the day, stretching outside porch or go to view of lake /ocean park

Connect with the source of guidance all around me: I invite all that is for my highest good to come and partner with me in this day toward loving mindful action (these two replace coffee for me)

In order to keep affirming self-care strategies on a daily basis I spend ten to twenty minutes, five days a week writing in a journal

This helps the inner critic to release tension as well as gives the inner artist a platform to express without edit — out comes poetry and haiku, snippets of song lyrics and melodies

I Take a Walk and call a friend somewhere in the middle of the day

Engage some creative outlet such as writing, art or play with guitar, keyboard, singing solo or with a friend 8-9 hours sleep daily

take 3 breaks a day stepping outside no matter the weather

Meals eating low processed foods, organic non-fried whenever possible

I take a soothing rest or a short nap (a long one if I can manage it on weekends).

WEEKLY

It was eight years ago that I built in 3-5 times a week I walk neighborhood and exercise at YMCA with a workout and swim, then treat myself to steam, sauna, or hot tub. For support I invite guests regularly.

I Prioritize and set up weekly individual meetings for tea or meal with friends on a growth path.

Arrange 4-8 hours a weekend for Deep moments / Solitude time — when I finally get to do a whole lot of nothing but relax into the flow of the moment!

I Sing, do vocal toning or Play music with another in a creative expression project which we often record, if even on our phones

I take a deep meditative walk or hike in a forested park or beach area with intention to commune with the life there and take in fresh air.

Attend a Support group such as a mindfulness meditation, yoga or men's group or can be 12 step, grief & loss or health care focus.

I Schedule one night at home each week without TV where options open up surprisingly like Taking a hot salt bath.

The above activities replace the need for lubricating alcohol drinks or other mind altering substances to relax.

MONTHLY

I pay a service provider to assist me in attending to my mental, emotional, and spiritual well-being: to a personal growth and development coach or a spiritual director or professional consultant and to two hours acupuncture / cranio sacral or massage.

I meet with a professional growth peer group for two hours which includes group meditation and visioning our life and work habits.

I take a three day weekend, each month, whether its a national holiday or I think I deserve it or not.

I am nourished by a day trip to state park or a few days at National park.

ANNUALLY

I set up a preventative health appointment with a medical doctor, as well as to a dentist and to Naturopath or specialist as needed.

I spend a Weekend at a retreat center where I review the year and see what served and what needs to be let go so something even more true to my path now can be enjoyed. Two weeks in a row off in summer - for a deep refresh and reset in the form of a vacation, pilgrimage, national park or stay-cation — or combination of them.

BEYOND: Schedule a Sabbatical every six to seven years where I engage a new book, cd recording and discern the right rule of life for the next 7 years

PART 2: EXERCISES & GUIDED MEDITATIONS

Timothy's daily morning intention-setting meditation to connect to the Source of all Life:

I reach down to touch the ground of my being, and touch earth as connected to all.

I invite all your support on the path;

all of my ancestors, wisdom teachers, guides, guardian angels

all who are for my highest good

to come,

and partner with me in my day.

As I make conscious contact with you deeper powers within me and around me.

May all this warm connection flow up into me, like hot lava love.

May the best of your and my qualities refill me now

so that I am

well supported, nurtured, nourished,

with confidence and conviction to follow path of love and serving.

Consider this meditatively while stretching or doing yoga, especially outside on the porch or deck with perspective on nature

<u>SONG:</u> An original meditation song to breathe in light and love to fill us up for the day ahead:

"Be filled (with light and love)," is number 6 on the cd or listen on Youtube: https://www.youtube.com/watch?v=AC9B- QOlqh4

with these lyrics after the chant gently guiding toward deeper refreshment with your life as it is:

> *Breathe, through your heart now, draw*
> *up from the Source. Settle into the*
> *ground of your very Being. Believing in*
> *yourself, Breathe in the Light, from the*
> *deepest power you know.*

> *Now be Filled with Light and Love:*
> *Breathe in Love through our hearts, Relax, Release,*
> *Be Freed from all that is no longer needed. Be Filled*
> *from the Love within, like Lava up through the*
> *Volcano, that is you, and out to the world that is*
> *suffering, confused, hurting, and often at war, with*
> *itself ...*
> *May Be all be filled with Light and Love*

<u>Reflection Questions for integration and next steps</u>:

Now its your turn: This is the moment when you put together all you have explored here into a trail map and a vision forward with support. We all have "growing edges" that we can lean into toward integrating throughout our life — new ones appear after the next development step was bravely taken. Another growth opportunity — oh, goody! So be gentle and see what emerges that calls to you from the deepest place you know.

1. First, of all the self-care strategies you have read about and written down what habits truly belong in your life? Make a loving list.

2. Where would like to plant these if they are not already part of your daily, weekly, monthly schedule?

3. What needs to be let go or released so that space emerges for new refreshment to be planted?

4. What resources and tools might affirm or remind you to take life-giving action?

5. Name a few people who you might share the above answers with and who might support you, (both personal connections and professionals)

6. Lastly, how might I schedule a meeting with regularly - another dedicated to refreshing their lives on a daily basis - or a mindfulness / self-care coach assist in this endeavor?

Conclusions:

A last word of support from my experience on the winding road of this interesting life: *What if you saw your life as largely uncharted territory with infinite choices that could each be lived "in the light," with the wind of inspiration and support at your back?* I laugh when I consider all the bumper stickers which say something like, "I would rather be _ golfing, shopping, fishing, etc."

A few years ago I created a bumper sticker online and put on my car - **"I'd rather be in the present moment."** Later that day a person walked up to me in a surprisingly frank encounter and said, *"thank you - that made my day. Honestly, so much of the time I feel like I should be somewhere else. Why can't I be happy with my life just as it is?"*

All I know is that when I take care of myself I feel happier. My life improves in myriad ways. Refreshment no longer eludes me. I get to truly come home to myself and to the truth that I have many choices. Lately, at the end of the day when I look in the mirror a voice within me whispers quietly, "I do accept myself as I am … from moment to moment. and it is enough.
In fact, I am enough. Thanks for tending to me today."

In closing, thank *you* for listening and opening yourself up to this exploration which we are engaging together. I honor your process of living into the quiet truth we often speak at the beginning of retreats: "You are exactly where you are supposed to be." Beginning again is humbling and freeing. So many possibilities open up for us from this vantage point. How exciting! As you continually seek refreshment and find your deeper connection in this life know I support you as a fellow traveler on the path. I trust you have all you need to grow this unique garden that is you. If I or another person in your community like me can support your courageous steps then let us know. We are here for you, courageous giver of care.

Addendum: What is 1:1 Spiritual Companioning / Direction?

Spiritual Direction, Accompaniment or Companioning is an age-old practice once reserved only for the elite, and those in monasteries. Now, all have the opportunity to reflect with a qualified spiritual director about one's life and its events with an eye to noticing where the Mystery or Spirit may be active, gently nudging us toward a fuller life and growth as a loving person. Though this style of spiritual support originated over 400 years ago in the Spiritual Exercises of St. Ignatius of Loyola (and in the 14th century treatise, "The Cloud of Unknowing," there are spiritual directors now around the world who represent almost every major religion (www.sdiworld.org)

And what and who is a "Director?"
A spiritual director is a companion on your spiritual journey who listens, supports, sometimes offers suggestions and practices yet is trained to tune into the true "director" animating the session. When we have a person focused entirely on our spiritual journey and practice for an hour we find treasures which we get to open up and explore. Often the greatest treat is we begin to recognize a larger purpose and Presence in our lives. In this sacred container we name and go beyond images of God we grew up to encounter the One beyond who is truly for our highest good. Many who begin this process stay in direction for years, for a lifetime. I have been accompanied this way for over 25 years myself, men and women, lay and ordained, spiritual disciplines coach and mentors.

What happens in a typical session?
A spiritual director helps the person to notice meaning and spirit in the circumstances of one's life. He or she will be listening, asking reflective questions and pointing out resources for meditation, daily prayer and/ or discernment to discover guidance to move forward with confidence. Often the session begins with some silence and a spoken prayer to center and ground ourselves. We assist with noticing resistances and roadblocks, helping the person to come to breakthroughs in their relationship with themselves and with the ultimate mystery. Tim sees people from a variety of faith traditions (or none at all) and ethnic backgrounds. He acts as a kind of bridge between west and east, in terms of practices he can suggest and traditions to explore.

How often do we meet -- and does it cost anything?
Sessions usually take place MONTHLY for an hour though initially meetings can be spaced as close as every two to three week, if helpful to form an adequate foundation and rappore. When monks and priest offered this service their communities covered all expenses so they could minister without fee. Today, most spiritual directors are not in religious life and thus need to make a living. Tim believes in setting up a sliding scale so as to make this service the most accessible to all income levels: between $50.00 - $85.00 hr. Tim also offers sessions by phone and via skype / other video conferencing, to persons as far as Austria and Costa Rica. See below for a combination of spiritual direction and energy clearing/healing/balancing.

Tim is a member of Spiritual Directors International and on the resource pools at Seattle University, Spiritual Exercises in Everyday Life (SEEL.org), Ignatian Spirituality Center (ignatiancenter.org) and a number of Retreat Centers on both coasts. His credential includes a Masters of Divinity from Seattle University and has a credential as a Spiritual Director Training Program through SEEL Puget Sound where he served as Retreat Leader in for students, faculty and staff at SU. and is available as consultant and offers supervision to other spiritual directors. Tim is an advisory board member with the Interfaith Council of Washington and resource for Baster University and University of Washington orientations.

Email at tim@timmalone.org to schedule an initial meeting to see if where you are at in your journey and how this might be a good fit at this time indoor journey. I trust that something larger is at work always in these connections toward growth - whether you choose to continue with me or desire referral to other source. See about other services I offer in conjunction with spiritual direction below.

HOW DO WE TAP INTO THE DEEP CONNECTION of peaceful healing power? Mindfulness coaching 1:1 is a way I guide people to practices.

Yet I am available to offer Sound Healing and Reiki / Healing Touch Techniques used in hospitals and clinics. Also, I am skilled to apply various alternative practices learned while apprenticing with healers-Shamans from as far as Bali which may help calm our overworked minds and hearts like a breath of fresh air let into our being. For medical studies on its benefits visit www.HealingtouchProgram.com or to learn about Reiki from Christian view.

Other publications by this Author

Guided Meditations Audio CD (due in May 2018): Companion to the Book

Tim Malone & Soul Fam: We are One CD

Sammy the Snake Monk of Siam: A Short Story

Articles in the Northwest Progress, 2004

Treasures Beyond Measure: One Year Solo Pilgrimage across Asia, Memoir (due in 2019)

I laugh at Myself, 1986, UNIVERSITY OF NOTRE DAME

Resurrection, 1996, in MEN'S JOURNAL Of Poetry

MEDIATIONS OF THE SEASON (Archdiocese.org archives)

Haiku & other mystical poetry — www.timmalone.org

Resources and Opportunities for Growth

PRH — Personal Growth and Development Programs for individuals and couples to discern their life path. PRHworld.org

Mindfulness Practice Centers around the Globe: www.plumvillage.org, at Stanford and UW.

Spiritual Directors International (Member and Certified) with a seek and find guide to practitioners

Centering Prayer - ContemplativeOutreach.org

Spiritual Exercises in Everyday Life: www.seelpugetsound.org and other versions of SEEL and CLC worldwide

Jesuit Center for Spiritual Growth, Wernersville PA, Maryland, and in almost every state (Including Jesuit Schools & Colleges)

IgnatianSpirituality.com and IgnatianCenter.org

Body awareness practices & spirituality www.Focusing.org,

The Twelve Steps of Alanon, Coda, ACA and AA

Seattle University School of Theology and Ministry

University of Notre Dame Developmental Psychology and Theology

Mindfulness / Coaching Trainings: Deer Park Monastery, Forest Monastery, Thailand; Bodhanath, Nepal; Empowerments at Dalai Lama's Meditation Centers in India; Soto Zen center, Kansai, Japan; Bali, Indonesia. Received 1:1 transmissions with Brother Wayne Teasdale and Willian Johnston Sophia University, Tokyo.

The Mystic Heart, Wayne Teasdale; Shantivanum & New Camaldolesce Monasteries, in Tamil Nadu and Big Sur, CA

The Artist's Way, by Julie Cameron

www.gratefulness.org

National Parks.org and Discover the Forest.org

ACKNOWLEDGMENTS

First, I wish to thank all my teachers and colleagues for formation and companionship over the span of my rich life: My dear Family and friends, health providers, my birth traditions, community of spiritual directors and mentors. I am grateful for this place, this space and the pace of life which facilitated this book to birth over the last two years. For the groups of explorers over many years who witnessed the emergence of words to a page and practiced the tools in the book in Magnolia, Burien, Seattle & Tacoma and the PA / D.C. area retreats. For Sabbatical spaces to write and edit the manuscript — Judy S., Karlene K.Wwebsite design/ photos Sandra Tjoa. I really could not have done it without the assistance of so many of you, and for sure, not without author Monica Elvig McDowell who walked me through the process and essentially midwifed this first book with me. A deep Bow of gratitude for unwavering support to my fellow artists, soul family in NW and budding writers on the path - you know who you are! And for Silent Bridge, who along with the One reminds me to dance with the flow like a wave while singing in the Wild …

ABOUT THE AUTHOR

of *Beyond WiFi: Find your Deeper Connection*

TIMOTHY MALONE, M.Div., is an Educator and facilitator for individuals, groups, and staffs on creative ways to apply soulful strategies and stress management practices into your busy lives. For the first half of his career he served as a vocational counselor in mental health clinics before acquiring a graduate degree at Seattle University where he trained as a spiritual director to lead retreats in more contemplative settings.

He then trained in skills of empathic listening, mindfulness and dozens of meditation practices from teachers and healers, Europe, Asia, and Polynesia from which the exercises of this book were gleaned. Over the last 20 years he has taught Continued education classes on World Religions as well as guest lectured from places as near as Seattle and Bastyr Universities to colleges in Thailand and Nepal while on sabbatical. Tim is not interested in being a spiritual guru but more of Tim the tool man, the go to guy for exploring practices that anchor you to be more present and open-hearted in your workplace, family and relationships.

He enjoys playing music that uplifts and spending time in creative expression amidst nature sanctuaries. He is available as a mindfulness and creativity coach as well as spiritual companioning /direction in person and by Skype/Facetime/Zoom. You can reach him at Tim@timmalone.org - or through his website chocked full of writings at Www.timmalone.org

I Have A Dream . . .

Out of the mud of human existence, every person becomes open and unfolded

like a lotus flower.

Because we each attend to our inner life

We find our spiritual home,

Each of us connecting to the Divine source

Daily

Within and around us.

And in this way

At this moment

We all may be One.

Written the year 2000: let us trust there is still hope for the new millenium

To shift and evolve our consciousness toward Love and Compassion daily.